Florida Move Guide

The Unofficial Moving To Florida
Warning, Decision and Help
Guide

Ron Stack

Florida Move Guide

The Unofficial Moving to Florida Warning, Decision and Help Guide

Second Edition

Copyright © 2013 by Ron Stack

All rights reserved.

Published in the United States of America

Printed in the United States of America

Published by Zeus Press Inc.

ZeusPress.com

ISBN 978-0-985-7792-0-7

Disclaimer

This book is presented to provide entertainment and information only. The author and publisher are not providing any financial, tax, legal, real estate or any other professional advice or services. While reasonable effort was used in putting this book together, the author and publisher make no representations or warranties of any kind as to the accuracy or completeness of the contents. The author and publisher assume no liability of any kind with respect to the books contents. No guarantees or warranties of any kind are expressed or implied in the book or by presenting it. The author and publisher shall not be held liable or responsible to any person or entity for any loss, incidental, consequential or otherwise, any damages caused, or alleged to have been caused, directly or indirectly, by the information presented. No warranty may be created or extended by anyone who is distributing, marketing or otherwise offering this book. You should seek the services of a competent professional for any financial, tax, legal, real estate or any other advice. You will be responsible for your decisions, choices and actions.

Table of Contents

Introduction

Most Florida Relocations Don't Last

A study published by the University of Florida in 2009 showed that more people moved out of Florida from 1980-2008 to live in another U.S. state, than the entire population of New Jersey today. In fact, the number of people who moved out of Florida during that time is greater than the total population now living in almost 40 U.S. States. The rate of people moving out of the sunshine is now more than 1,000 a day.

I know you probably find that hard to believe. In the mid 1990s as I was making a "permanent" move to the sunshine state, if someone had told me I would come to dislike the place so much that I would move out, I would have told them they were dead wrong. I had been to Florida so many times on vacation I thought I knew all there was to know about the place. I always had a great time and had to move there.

The first couple of months in Florida were like living in paradise. It was like being on a long vacation. I often asked myself why I waited so long to make the move. Within a year, however, that feeling started to wear off. Things that I never experienced or noticed while on vacation started to appear.

Before I moved to Florida, I had no idea so many people ended up moving back or what their reasons were. That never came up in any of the research I did. How could moving to Florida possibly be a mistake? Simply put, living here is a lot different than spending a vacation here. On vacations, you don't experience everything you will once you live here every day.

When I started working as a realtor in Florida, I was surprised by all the calls from sellers that wanted to sell and get out of Florida. They said they made a huge mistake moving there. At first I didn't completely understand their frustration, but the longer I lived in Florida, the more I understood how they felt.

Reasons for Moving Back Home

The reasons given for moving back home were many, but as I talked to more sellers, I realized that several of the same ones were mentioned by nearly everyone. That is what this book is about. It's about the reasons given by hundreds of sellers whose "permanent" move plans had changed after actually living in Florida. Living in Florida turned out to be something far different for them than the paradise they moved here for.

Why did I wish I knew about all this before I moved?

Florida Move Mistake's High Cost

Selling your home to move to Florida is costly. Moving a thousand miles away is expensive. Buying another home means paying more costs. A move like this is a big disruption to enjoying life, but we do it because we think life will improve. Can you imagine losing all that money and going through the hassle just to realize you made a mistake and have to do it all over again to move back home?

Regardless of whether you own now or are renting, moving long distances costs a lot of money. The stress and misery caused can be even costlier. Working as a real estate agent, people have told me the stress of two long distance moves, multiple home sales and the financial loss caused divorces, bankruptcy and even heart attacks.

The Purpose of the Book

Am I trying to talk you out of moving to Florida? Absolutely not. I am still a licensed real estate broker in the state of Florida as I write this update. There are people who have moved here, and it worked out well for them, long term. The purpose of this book is to give you an idea of what living in Florida is really like, and why millions of people who made a permanent move here moved out.

This is not a fiction book or one based on theories. I will share with you the actual reasons given by hundreds of sellers for their permanent move to paradise that turned into a disaster. My hope is that, as you read this book, you can determine if you are more likely to enjoy living in Florida long term, or if you can see how some of the reasons that have forced millions out of Florida may affect you as well. My only agenda is to try to help the people who may move to Florida only to discover it was a mistake, from making that mistake in the first place.

The other purpose of this book is to help those who are moving to Florida to increase their chances of a successful long term relocation with help on how to minimize the problems that have chased others from the state. Why did a permanent move work for some? I will share that with you, as well as tips of where to live, what homes to buy and what to avoid.

1. Evacuations and Hurricanes

You Can't Know This Until You Live it

You have just moved to Florida after selling your comfortable home up north that you've had for years. It's been a couple of months since the move, and your new place is finally starting to feel like home. The first month was hectic. It was lot of work setting up a new home. Back home, your family would have helped you move, but you live too far away for that now.

It's a beautiful evening. You decide to relax while watching a TV show with your wife before going to bed. Suddenly, the show is interrupted for a special emergency update. The National Hurricane Center has moved the "cone of uncertainty" of an approaching hurricane over your area. Worse yet, a hurricane hunter aircraft now reports the storm offshore has strengthened to a category two and further strengthening is expected. They also report that growing into the most destructive category 5 is not impossible as this hurricane picks up strength from the warm coastal waters just before landfall. They expect it to hit land the day after tomorrow. Mandatory evacuations have just been announced for your area tomorrow starting at eight o'clock in the morning. Huh?

Forced to Leave Your Home

You are told you should prepare to leave immediately and secure your home before you do. They again warn that this is a mandatory evacuation. If you leave too late, the winds may down trees and power lines and prevent you from getting out. They warn you that if you choose to stay, any call for help does not have to be legally responded to because doing so would put the few remaining emergency personnel at risk. That is why you must leave.

All of a sudden, it hits you. For the first time in your life, you are being ordered to leave your home. Where will you go? How long will you be gone? Will your home still be here when you return?

It's getting late. It's dark outside but it's still hot and humid. Like most of Florida, in this part of paradise you chose for retirement, September still means hot, humid nights. You would be attacked by swarms of mosquitoes if you went outside now and started putting up your hurricane shutters. You made sure the house you bought came with them, but you've been too busy moving that you haven't had time to figure out how to put them up. You now wonder if you even have the tools needed. How heavy are those metal things anyway? It's supposed to be ninety-three degrees and humid tomorrow, how long will it take?

You have so much to do before you pack up and leave, but it's getting late and you are both tired and stressed. You both agree on getting a good night's sleep and starting early in the morning on what must be done. You turn in.

This news has upset your spouse so much she says she can't sleep and might as well start packing. This is difficult for her. What precious items do you take, and what do you leave behind that you may never see again? There are far too many family pictures, heirlooms and other prized sentimental possessions to fit everything in the car.

No Place to Go

You decide to make reservations for a place to stay safe from the storm. After trying online and then by phone, you give up. With almost half a million people evacuating with you, there are no rooms left anywhere within a couple hundred miles. The travel agency promises to call if they can come up with anything.

Gas! You've heard of gas shortages happening when all those extra cars are on the road. You tell your wife you're going to fill up now. It's late, and maybe there won't be any lines. You will be right back.

As you get close to the nearest gas station, you see long lines have already formed. You call home to say it's going to take a while, but you'll be home as soon as you can.

As you sit in line, you think about all the things you have to do tomorrow. Put up the hurricane shutters. Move all the lawn ornaments, lanai furniture and anything else that might become a projectile when picked up by 100+ mph winds, and put them into the garage. Where will you put it all? You're tired, and the more you think about it, the more stress you feel.

The horror of living through another hurricane season with the threat of evacuations or total destruction of your home is one of the main reasons given for leaving the state. Most have never experienced this while on vacation here. It's something most prospective Floridians never think about. The truth is, even those who considered it couldn't imagine what it is really like to be under threat six months a year, every year of losing everything you have. You have to live here and experience it to realize the toll it can take. That is how most of the issues that force people to leave Florida work. You really don't realize what it's like until you live here and are forced to go through it.

Hurricane season starts June 1st and ends November 30th. The hype of danger by the media starts even before the season does. It starts with warnings to get your "hurricane kit" together. When a hurricane hits, it can destroy thousands of homes, but it can also knock out power and utilities for a million people, far away from the worst destruction. That's why you need this kit. Bottled water because you won't get it from your spigot after the storm hits. Canned food because the stores won't be open and the refrigerators won't work. Flashlights, batteries and candles because there won't be any power for light. The worst part, hurricane season happens during Florida's six months of hot, humid summer, and unless you have a whole house generator and fuel, living without AC is barbaric. The point is to be prepared to live without access to food, water, electric and anything you might want from a store for weeks or months.

How Hurricane Sandy That Hit the Northeast in 2012 Compares

The hurricane that slammed the coastal areas of New Jersey and New York and left many without power in numerous states lost its category 1 hurricane status just before landfall. Florida regularly gets hit by category 2-5 storms that are far more powerful and destructive than Sandy.

Evacuations Ordered More Often

Evacuations can be even worse than hurricanes, because although your Florida home may never be leveled by a hurricane, you may have to go through multiple evacuations in certain years. They are more likely now, after Hurricane Katrina devastated New Orleans in 2005. Evacuations prior to that came late or not at all. They failed to order widespread evacuations prior to hurricane Katrina making landfall. That storm surprised emergency planners and people suffered. After the world watched days of TV footage showing thousands of desperate citizens trapped in the Superdome without adequate food, water and restroom facilities for a long period of time, the authorities now err on the side of caution. You are now less likely to be in your home when a hurricane hits which is a good thing, but you are also more likely to be told you must evacuate and leave it.

I've seen the aftermath of a hurricane up close with my own eyes. You can be trapped in a home with no air conditioning in the Florida summer heat and humidity. Trapped because the streets will be littered with downed trees and telephone poles, electrical wires and roofs that make using your car or truck to get out impossible.

For thousands of former residents, their dream of moving to Florida to relax and enjoy the warm weather ended when they lost their home and all their personal possessions. After Hurricane Charley landed in Florida as the first of the record-setting 2004 season, I ventured out after a few weeks to see the damage. Seeing the devastation with your own eyes and standing on the ground where the destruction occurred is completely different than a two minute piece on the 6 o'clock news. It looked like a war zone that had been nuked. There were large areas where the homes didn't have roofs anymore. It was like a giant weed whacker went through and cut all the homes, power lines and trees in half. Furniture, family photos, kids' toys were mixed in with the debris among downed tree and power lines.

One of the main complaints from those that decided to leave the state was the stress they went through every time a storm was named. Watching constant emergency updates and worrying until the storm makes land fall or is no longer a threat takes its toll. Most hurricanes move at the rate of 10-15 mph and are tracked from the time they are just a tropical storm far out in the Gulf or Atlantic Ocean. This is well before the authorities can determine where it is likely to go. You will hear about each named storm for days, maybe even weeks.

The names given to storms each year start over with A and go in alphabetical order. In October 2005, hurricane Wilma (yes, with a W) finally hit Florida after wandering aimlessly out in the Atlantic for over a week. That was the end of a second year in a row of a record number of hurricanes that made landfall and for destruction caused.

Preparing Your Home Before You Evacuate

The tricky part about this is the timing. You don't want to bring your outside stuff in too early because if the "cone of danger" moves away from your area, you wasted your time. Keep in mind this will not be pleasant. Hurricane season happens in the 6 months of a Florida summer (yes, summer in Florida is not three short months, more on that latter), and it's hot and humid. You also don't want to wait too long because moving that stuff when the hurricane is too close can be next to impossible with wind gusts strong enough to blow you around and frequent violent thunderstorms and rain bands.

The next issue you must decide on during this prep time is your hurricane shutters. Most new homes in the lower to middle price ranges are sold with metal hurricane shutters. They are usually stacked together neatly in the garage bolted to a wall. You are to take these and put them up around all the openings of your home such as windows and doors. Again, it's all about timing. You have to be extra careful about this because although they are not light, if you try to put them up in strong winds they could blow right out of your hands. If you thought about hiring someone to do it for you, good luck. Thousands of others have that same idea and getting someone is next to impossible.

You could put them up early, but once you do, your home will become like a cave. No light gets in. When all the shutters are up, you can't tell if its midnight or sunny outside. It's just dark inside your home in the Sunshine State.

That's why some people put them up and take them down for every threat regardless of the hassle. A growing number are getting tired of that and putting them up when the first threat comes and leaving them up for the whole season. Choosing to live in the dark over constantly putting them up and taking them down is a choice that some people make if their community doesn't have restrictions against that. Homes with metal shutters, or worst yet plywood shutters, up for weeks or months are not a pretty site.

There are other options like clear shutters, electric or crank down ones and shatter proof windows (aka hurricane or impact resistant windows). They're more costly but offer more convenience. They do have drawbacks, but all that will be covered in a later chapter.

While you are coordinating the shutters and the outside stuff, you also have to be ready to implement your evacuation plan. Fill the gas tank early because the pumps can go dry when hundreds of thousands of people are ordered to leave their home and make an unplanned trip. You don't want to run out of gas on the interstate in a hurricane traffic jam.

What Doesn't Fit in the Car, Lost Forever?

When ordered to leave your home, you have to decide what possessions you cherish most, and what will fit in the car. Anything you leave behind could be lost forever. I always kept a list of what I was going to take, and where they were located. It was a lot easier that way because I didn't have think about it, I just packed.

Waiting until an evacuation is ordered to travel makes it more difficult. You will have the company of thousands, possibly hundreds of thousands of people that must do the same thing. It may be impossible to get reservations for any place to stay anywhere within a day's drive. During the summer, tourists can already have most hotels well booked up.

I had a couple of hotels in the center of the state picked out to evacuate to because they had very good cancellation policies. I made reservations whenever there was even a possibility a hurricane might threaten my area. I would cancel without a charge if they weren't needed. Having the hotel picked out, phone numbers and travel directions handy meant I had less to think about when an emergency approached.

Another complaint of waiting until an evacuation is ordered is the travel. The roads taking you out of harm's way can become a nightmare. Expect ten mph stop and go, bumper to bumper traffic that causes lots of fender benders to make things worse. Since this involves so many more cars on the road than usual, gas stations run out of gas. People also hoard gas during this time for their home generators in case of long power outages after the storm.

You may be stuck idling in stopped traffic on the interstate with your gauge on empty. You may be lucky enough to get off at the next exit before you run out of gas only to find that gas stations have no gas left. Cars without gas clog the roads. Fender benders, exhausted and stressed out people on the side of the road in the heat, humidity and rain, it's not a great place to be.

If you leave long before any evacuation order, you can avoid all of that. If the hurricane changed course and an evacuation was never ordered, I just looked at it like a short vacation. I didn't miss much during those few days because not many people want to look at real estate in an area that has a hurricane heading that way.

Some have told me they leave late, after everybody else and the roads are clear. I would not suggest this because when a major hurricane is even a hundred miles away, you can have blinding rain and wind gusts that will blow your car around. Driving at interstate speed and suddenly not being able to see anything because of the amount of rain pounding the windshield is not fun.

If you need to work to support a family, consider what the effect hurricane season could have on your income. Preparing for a hurricane and evacuating your home can be disruptive to your paycheck. On top of that, you have the extra cost of gas, accommodations and meals out. If you are on a fixed retirement income or work to support a young growing family and are living paycheck to paycheck, an evacuation could cause financial indigestion.

Hurricane Consideration Time

Hurricanes and life disrupting evacuations were a major reason given by many people for their decision to move out of Florida. This usually happens after or during a particularly active storm season, but some can't handle the stress, even during relatively quiet years. There are years when Florida seems to be a hurricane magnet and other years when the state seems to have been sprayed with storm repellant. The question isn't if another hurricane will hit Florida, but when will it be and what area?

If you are retiring and looking for a place to relax, ask yourself if you want to move somewhere you'll have to deal with hurricane season for six months every year. Do you want to see your wife or husband try to decide what sentimental things to pack into the car and what to leave behind that could be lost forever? How will you feel when you're told you must leave your home, even it's for your own safety? Are you prepared to intentionally put yourself and your family in a home that you could be repeatedly forced to leave, or have it totally destroyed?

How and When Tropical Storms and Hurricanes Form

The Atlantic Hurricane season that affects Florida runs from June 1ˢᵗ until November 30ᵗʰ, officially half a year. In recent years, June, July and August have been fairly tame. The media hypes things up, and there are storms going on out in the Atlantic that meteorologists warn about, but rarely do they amount to a storm that actually hits Florida and causes any disruption or damage. That said, hurricanes have landed and caused destruction during the early part of the season, so no storm threat should be ignored.

Tropical storms and hurricanes that threaten Florida are born from the Gulf of Mexico or more commonly the Atlantic Ocean when the waters are warm enough for them to form. Hurricanes can't form out of chilly water, so that is why there are no hurricane threats in the winter when the water surrounding Florida is much cooler.

How These Storms Affect the Quality of Life in Florida

Media Coverage

The media announces hurricane season every year and will devote extra time to covering how to "assemble a hurricane kit" type stories. When a storm forms far out in the water, even if it's a week away from coming anywhere near Florida, expect a lot of extra face time for the meteorologists, especially for the first few storms of the season.

If the long range projected path for a named storm is anywhere near your part of Florida, you can expect almost continuous news coverage. Hurricanes can travel at a very slow 15 mph and change direction, and then change back. Hurricanes are devastating, so I can understand the coverage, but my experience has been that even if the projected path is moved right at you, but it's still five days away, the path will likely change and the day it impacts somewhere far away, it could be a perfect weather day where you are. This can be nerve racking for some, especially the first few times.

Tip: Pay attention, but don't let early coverage of named storms a week or more away consume you. Play closer attention if the projected path includes your area five days from landfall and very close

23

attention if you are still in the cone of uncertainty four days from impact.

Evacuations

A bad evacuation experience can cause a Florida resident, new or otherwise, to move to a state that is not affected by hurricanes. Your chances of being forced to leave your home if you live along the coast like most Florida residents do, is much higher than your chances of ever having major damage to your home.

Tip: Have a list of what to do to prepare your home for evacuation, before you need it. Have a list of what you will pack to take with you when you evacuate, including the most precious items that you would not want to lose if your home would be destroyed. Know exactly where you will evacuate to, before hurricane season begins.

Storm Surge

Storm surge is a wall of water that is carried onto land by a hurricane. The height of this wall can be higher than the highest point of your roof. There is nothing you can do to specifically protect your home from storm surge except live far enough away from the coast to be affected, or build a stilt home to live in.

The idea behind stilt homes is that the water will flow under the living areas of the home that is built high off the ground to lower the risk of damage. Today, luxury stilt homes built along the coast are often built with elevators to whisk you to the living area level. They are not for people with modest budgets but may be the only option for building in some coastal areas or barrier islands.

Regardless of what type of home you live in, if storm surge is a strong possibility from an oncoming hurricane, you will likely be subject to a mandatory evacuation. Having a stilt home just means you may have a home to come back to.

Tip: Look at storm surge maps for the area that you are considering so you know the risk before you even start looking at homes. A home's risk of destruction from storm surge will have a big effect on insurance rates. A home in a high risk area may make the cost of insurance impossible to afford or even obtain in the future, which could be two years after you buy it (more on insurance later). A separate flood insurance policy may be required to be compensated for any claim from storm surge.

Flooding

Unusually heavy rains can affect areas far away from where a hurricane or tropical storm will make landfall, and long before it arrives. Flooding can occur quickly in high hazard flood zones or just about anywhere a tropical system is dumping rain far faster than you may have ever experienced before moving to Florida.

Tip: Buy the newest home you can (more likely to be subject to newer building codes and built to minimize flood damage) and avoid high risk flood zones. Consider obtaining flood insurance even if you aren't required to. Flood insurance is cheap compared to the risk now, but the program likely will be restructured in the future to better reflect the risk so that taxpayers aren't continually asked to bailout the fund to pay for homeowners that repeatedly rebuild in high hazard locations.

Note: Avoiding high risk flood zones may sound like a no brainer, but Florida is surrounded by water on three sides, and most land is barely above sea level and flat. All areas of Florida are subject to tropical storm systems and heavy rain. There are many populated areas located entirely in a flood plain, so avoiding high risk flood areas may not be as easy as it sounds.

Wind Damage

When a tropical disturbance attains sustained winds of 39 mph, it then becomes a tropical storm and is given a name. The practice of naming storms started in 1956 to make it easier to keep track of them when there are more than one happening at a time. A tropical storm becomes a category one hurricane when sustained winds reach 74 mph. As the sustained winds increase, so does the category of the hurricane until it reaches category five at 132 mph, the highest.

Building codes in Florida have been strengthened over the years to make homes more resistant to the effects of storms. There are many different types of hurricane protection for a home's windows. The least expensive options require a lot of time and labor to put up and take down.

Tip: When moving to Florida, be sure you have

hurricane hardened doors, including the outside garage door and window protection. Any door or window that breaks or gets blown open and allows high winds to enter, increases the chance of the roof being blown off and heavy rains to enter. Impact resistant windows are a pricier solution, but once installed, you won't have the hassle of putting up and taking down shutters in high winds, heat and humidity. The windows also increase your safety from crime by making it nearly impossible for an intruder to break in through a window. Other types of hurricane protection can block out all sunlight and detract from the appearance of your home.

Blackouts or loss of electric power

It's quite possible to return from a mandatory evacuation because of a hurricane to a home that has little or no damage, but no power. Because of downed trees, power lines and damage to the grid, homes far from where most of the destruction happened can be without power for days, weeks or months. Few things in modern life can be as frustrating as living without electric for days. Not having hot water for showers, or air conditioning during hot muggy Florida weather, or a working refrigerator, lights, cable, TV, or internet connection will turn your life into a miserable third world existence.

Consider having a whole home power back up system installed for your home. They are not cheap, but they automatically turn on when needed and can power everything in your home including the AC. If your budget doesn't allow that, get a portable generator soon after moving to Florida. They can be hard to get after a storm when thousands of people in your area need one.

How to Minimize or eliminate the Effects of Hurricane Seasons on Your Florida Lifestyle

There is a way to live in Florida and minimize most of hurricane season's effects upon your life. Hurricanes that affect Florida are born over warm water. They need the warm water to survive and strengthen. Once a hurricane makes landfall, it starts to weaken because it no longer has the warm gulf or ocean water to feed it. As hurricanes move inland, they lose their strength and eventually become just a bad storm. Coastal areas are where most of the destruction occurs. If you move to an area in the middle of the state, you would never experience the kind of devastation that happens on the coast where storms make landfall. Your chance of ever having to go through a mandatory evacuation is far lower if you lived in Gainesville or Orlando, for instance, than anywhere along the coast. In fact, I've stayed in both of those places to ride out hurricane threats when I lived on the coast.

Hurricanes, evacuations and the hassles that come with living along the Florida coast during busy storm seasons has caused many people (possibly millions) to move out of Florida over the years. There are years when hurricanes are little or no real threat to the state. No one really knows what will happen during your first hurricane season in the state.

Something to think about

If you can see how hurricanes and evacuations could cause such a disruption to life that it would cause people who made a permanent move to Florida move back home, chances are it could happen to you too. You could drastically lesson the possibility of storm disruption to your Florida lifestyle by:

1) Moving to the center of the state.

2) Living in the newest home that appeals to you that you can afford (built in 2005 or later).

3) Choosing an area that is not a high hazard food zone.

4) Having impact resistant (hurricane) windows and doors so you don't have to fool with putting shutters up and down or living in a home without sunlight.

5) Having a whole home power back up system.

If you're saying to yourself, move to the center of the state, is he crazy? What about the beach? If you want to maintain your love for the beach, move to the center of the state and visit the beach a few times a year. If you want to turn your love for it into disdain, live near the beach and go there every day for years.

Love Florida's theme parks? Visit them sparingly and maintain that desire. What to kill the love? Move near the theme park and get a cheap Florida resident pass that allows unlimited visits. Go there all the time. Too much of what you want becomes what you don't want for most people, and that includes the beach and theme parks.

A hurricane off the coast of Florida as seen from space. Photo provided by NASA.

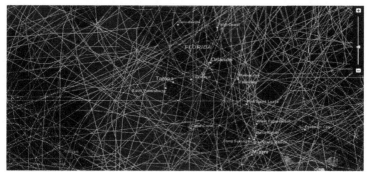

A historical map of the tracks of past hurricanes. When you move to Florida, the question is not "if" you will be affected by hurricanes, but when, how often and to what extent.

A great tool is available from NOAA that allows you to enter the area you were thinking of relocating to and see the paths of past hurricanes that affected the area. http://maps.csc.noaa.gov/hurricanes/

Hurricane Facts

Every second, a major hurricane unleashes energy equivalent to multiple atomic bombs.

In 1999, Hurricane Floyd, just a category 1 on the 1-5 hurricane scale, destroyed 19 million trees while causing $1,000,000,000 in damage.

Jupiter, a planet much larger than the Earth, has a hurricane the size of Earth that has been going on for over 300 years.

"Interesting Hurricane Facts" April 11, 2011 6:41:15 PM. April 11, 2011. http://www.hurricane-facts.com/Interesting-Hurricane-Facts.php

2. Missing Family Friends Home

Holidays without Family or Friends

Most of the people I helped to buy homes in Florida moved there from another state or country. Many moved from an area they had lived in most of their lives. They learned to drive, went on their first date and got their first job there. Most said they liked the place they moved from, but based on visits to Florida, they felt that a move there would improve their lives. Why else would any sane person spend a fortune and endure the hassles of a long distance move to another state?

I met a nice couple we'll call Bob and Mary when they moved from Michigan and bought a home from me here in Florida. They had lived in the same area outside of Detroit all of their lives. They dreamed of moving to Florida for years because they vacationed here many times and always loved it. They thought moving to Florida to escape the cold Michigan winters was a great idea. So when Bob retired from the plant, they made the decision to move.

Bob and Mary put their home in Michigan up for sale. They had lived in the home for over two decades. They raised their three children there, but now the kids were now all out on their own. Two of them had children of their own but all lived within an hour of the old homestead.

There were a lot of wonderful family memories in that home, Mary later told me. Every year at Thanksgiving, Christmas and other holidays, all of the kids and grandchildren would gather and spend most of the day at their home. It was like "home base."

The home they bought in Florida was not far from where they spent many vacations. Their new home was less than 10 minutes to the beach, had a pool and there were dozens of golf courses within a short drive. Everything seemed perfect. It was working out just like they planned, and they were happy those first few months.

As the first set of holidays since their move approached, Mary decided it might be a good time to start making plans for Thanksgiving. Everybody always came to their home for the holiday, and she was hoping that would continue. Mary loved preparing a big family meal and seeing everybody together again.

They now lived over 1000 miles away from the kids and grandkids, so new arrangements would have to be made. Mary made calls back home to invite everybody down to their new home for Thanksgiving. She thought the idea of spending the holiday where it was warm would be appealing.

The kids were not as enthusiastic as she had hoped. They would have to take additional time off from work. The grandkids had school. Their kids' spouses had planned to spend time with their parents in Michigan like usual, and it was kind of expected. Everybody promised they would discuss it and let her know.

Over the next couple of weeks, Mary learned that because of other commitments, only one family said they could make it. She was a little upset. Although she usually talked to the kids and grandkids every week, she hadn't seen them since the move, and she really missed them. Still, she was looking forward to seeing her one son, his wife and the two little ones, even if it would only be for a couple of days.

Mary had been experiencing mixed emotions about the move, but never said anything to Bob. They had met some of the neighbors which they said were all nice, but they didn't really connect with any of them. They had friends back home that they were very comfortable with, some they had known for decades. She was feeling kind of lonely and really looking forward to this Thanksgiving with family.

The week before the holiday, her son called and told her the grandkids had gotten the flu, so they weren't going to be able to make it. Bob told me that Mary wasn't the same after that. When Bob and Mary sat down to a Thanksgiving meal by themselves, Mary began to cry. That's the first time she told Bob that she thought moving to Florida may have been a mistake, and she wanted to move back.

New Doctor, Dentist, Hair Stylist, Everything

Most people never think about having to find someone new just to cut their hair. Before I moved to Florida, I went to the same place and had my hair cut by the same person for fifteen years. I looked the same for a decade and a half. After my first haircut in Florida, I looked like a fresh Army recruit. A couple of months later when my hair grew back, the thought of getting a haircut at another strange place made chills go down my spine. I decided to try the place that had a big "we fix cheaper haircuts" sign out front. The result? Another bad haircut, only this time it cost twice as much.

It took me years to find a place that provided a dental experience I was comfortable with. Then the dentist retired and sold to a dentist fresh out of school. Everything changed, so I had to look for someone new again.

I lucked out on finding a doctor shortly after I settled in Florida that was similar to the doctor I had for decades back home. Unfortunately, this doctor had decided to move back to the state he came from and the office was vacant after he left.

Most of the people you'll meet after moving to Florida, are not from the sunshine state originally. Your neighbors, the professional service providers you use and shop owners are more likely to have moved to Florida from another state or country just like you did, and could move back at any time. Since most people who move to Florida will at some point move back out, be prepared for a higher level of change of faces, names and places than you may be accustomed to.

More Time, More Courses, but Lost Desire

I once got a call from a man who wanted to sell his home after living in Florida for less than a year. Golf was one of his favorite activities in his life. After he retired, he convinced his reluctant wife to sell a home they lived in for 35 years in New York and move to Florida where golf is played year round.

The area they moved to was a paradise for golf fanatics. It had many more courses than where he lived up north and they were lush and green all year. They bought a place right on the fairway of a great course.

This guy joined a few organizations and volunteered at a couple of others to meet other golfers he might enjoy playing a round with. After a while, he realized he just didn't click with any of the new people the way he did with his long time golf buddies up north. They didn't have the same sense of humor. They couldn't be counted on to show up regularly. The members of the group changed constantly and sometimes no one showed up at all. After almost a year, he realized that one of the things he enjoyed about golf so much was socializing with a great group of long-time friends.

This guy now lived on a beautiful lush golf course surrounded by many more. The weather allowed him to play all year long. He lived in a golfer's paradise, but he no longer enjoyed the game. His wife was never thrilled about the move in the first place, and she missed the grand kids. They decided they were moving back home.

Living Near Family or Friends in Florida

If you are moving to Florida and will be near family or old friends, the chances of your move working out long term likely will be much higher. One example was a couple who bought a home from me for when they retire, which was still a few years off. They came down for vacations in the meantime and often brought family and friends with them. Over the next few years, three other couples from back home also bought future retirement homes and all on the same street as the first couple. When they all do move here full time they will be surrounded with friends and family in their new state.

Another successful move to a more tropical climate started with a job transfer. This young couple called on a home I had advertised for sale. They were married and had one small child. The husband was transferred from Illinois to the territory I sold in. I found them a home in a nice, quiet, safe area with good public schools. Shortly after they closed on the home and moved in, they called to tell me that the wife's parents were in town and they were interested in looking for a possible relocation.

While showing homes to the parents, I learned the daughter that moved here was an only child. So when she moved away, they immediately started to miss their only daughter and grandchild. They bought a place near their daughter and moved down. Over the next couple of years, I was contacted to help find homes for different members of the husband's family as well. In the following years when whenever I run into them at a restaurant or store, they always seemed to be with some of their extended family. They have told me how glad they were to have made the move. Living near other family members was one of the main reasons why.

I'm not suggesting that the only way to ensure a move to Florida will work long term is living near friends and family, but it helps. I've noticed many newcomers expect to quickly meet people and make new friends, and that does sometimes happen, but it takes effort. However, many have told me that finding people they can really bond with like long time friends from back home was more difficult than they anticipated.

Of course, there are people who move down and don't really miss anyone or anything from back home. If you're not a part of a large, close family or you dread the couple of times a year you do see relatives, a long distance move may be perfect for you. If the only time you see the in-laws is on Christmas day and a big fight always breaks out, you may not miss that.

If you have family or friends that live in Florida, moving near them can greatly increase your chances of long term satisfaction with your move. You'll have others to share holidays with, and they can tell you what doctors, hairdressers, etc. they use.

Leaving Home

When you moved from one home to another in your home state, it was probably a great experience. Your family and friends were still close. You worked at the same job. You were still close enough to get together with friends you've had for a long time. When moving to a larger home or downsizing in the same area, the home changes, but everything else stays the same. That's not true when you move a thousand miles away.

Has any member of your family expressed concerns of leaving where you now live? If anyone in your family has a serious issue with moving to Florida, make sure they feel comfortable with expressing their feelings about it before moving. Any serious concerns about moving should be addressed to see if they are just normal fears of the unknown or whether they run deeper. A concealed fear or bad attitude about moving can fester after the move to Florida, and surface as a problem that can only be solved by moving back home.

Many people who had a strong feeling they wouldn't

like Florida but kept it hidden to please someone else, or because they felt they had no choice became so miserable after the move, they forced a move back. Talking with all family members and making sure they feel free to express any concerns about moving so far away may prevent this. It's better to discover and address potential relocation problems before the move.

For instance:

1) A spouse who expresses a concern about missing the kids, grandkids or other family.

2) A child who fears living in a new area without friends, starting a new school, etc.

3) A spouse with a serious medical condition who has had the same trusted doctors for years and worries that losing them may worsen their condition.

4) Does anyone have strong vital friendships or community ties they feel may be impossible to replace? Do you have a child who excels in a program like football or band, and has been with the same group of kids year after year? A spouse that has attained a special role as a volunteer or in a social network?

Many of the people you'll meet in Florida aren't from the state originally and may be leaving at some point in the future. A strong sense of community is not easy to come by. Chances are the area you move to will be far more transient than you've ever experienced before. Expecting the same social support and stability in Florida may lead to disappointment and a desire to move back.

Based on hundreds of conversations with people moving in and out of Florida, this is what I've observed:

1) If you're happy with where you live now but are moving to Florida to improve on that, you may not find that overall improvement and regret the move.

2) If you are moving to Florida mainly to escape three or four months of winter, after being there a few years you may find you despise six to nine months of muggy, humid weather each year even more.

3) If you're truly unhappy with where you live now, moving to Florida may work out long term.

There are lifestyle options discussed later in the book that can eliminate most of Florida's full-time living issues.

How plans for frequent travel back home usually work out

Many plan to solve the separation from family and friends by making frequent trips back home, often for holidays. Many do follow through in the beginning but end up dreading the travel as the years go by. Ask any experienced road-warrior. Frequent travel can become brutal, especially around the holidays. If you plan on driving, living in the northern part of Florida will make the trips easier. Living in the Jacksonville area compared to Tampa, for instance, can shorten driving time by four hours each way. It's always the last few hours of an all day drive that are the worst. It can also make the difference between doing in just one day or having to get a hotel room.

Living close to an airport makes flying less of a hassle, of course, and many airlines have ridiculously low airfares flying from large cities like Orlando but also from lesser known airports. If you plan on flying frequently, a quick check of flights and fares may help in choosing what part of Florida to relocate to if you haven't already chosen.

A Grandfather's Love By Sara Teasdale

They said he sent his love to me,

They wouldn't put it in my hand,

And when I asked them where it was,

They said I couldn't understand.

I though they must have hidden it,

I hunted for it all the day,

And when I told them so at night,

They smiled at turned their heads away.

They say that love is something kind,

That I can never see or touch.

I wish he'd sent me something else,

I like his cough drops twice as much.

Florida Commercial Airports

Daytona Beach	DAB	Daytona Beach International Airport
Fort Lauderdale	FLL	Fort Lauderdale–Hollywood International Airport
Fort Myers	RSW	Southwest Florida International Airport
Gainesville	GNV	Gainesville Regional Airport
Jacksonville	JAX	Jacksonville International Airport
Key West	EYW	Key West International Airport
Melbourne	MLB	Melbourne International Airport
Miami	MIA	Miami International Airport
Orlando	MCO	Orlando International Airport
Orlando	SFB	Orlando Sanford International

		Airport
Panama City Beach	ECP	Northwest Florida Beaches International Airport
Pensacola	PNS	Pensacola International Airport
Punta Gorda	PGD	Punta Gorda Airport
Sarasota / Bradenton	SRQ	Sarasota–Bradenton International Airport
St. Augustine	UST	Northeast Florida Regional Airport
St. Petersburg	PIE	St. Petersburg–Clearwater International Airport
Tallahassee	TLH	Tallahassee Regional Airport
Tampa	TPA	Tampa International Airport
Valparaiso	VPS	Northwest Florida Regional Airport / Eglin Air Force Base
West Palm Beach	PBI	Palm Beach International Airport

3. You Can't Escape This

Longer, More Humid Summers

I've talked to lots of prospective new Floridians and warm weather is a main reason people move to Florida. A lot of newcomers are under the impression that Florida is hot during the summer, and then pleasantly "warm" the rest of the year. I guarantee you there is no place in Florida like that. Most of Florida is warm during the winter and hot and muggy the rest of the year.

Real estate agents and brokers make a living selling homes. After spending a fortune on advertising, they won't try to talk buyers out of buying a home but should always be honest with a buyer. When I was asked, "how long does this humidity last?" by buyers in the summer, and I would say seven to nine months a year in this area, I could tell most didn't believe me.

When asked the same question in October when it was still 84 degrees with high humidity and it feel like ninety, it was more believable.

While visiting in September when it still felt like 92 degrees every day, home shoppers would tell me the heat was not that bad. Of course, many are at the beach or in the hotel pool cooling off much of the day too. They look lobster- red after only a few days. You can't do that every day of the year if you live here, unless you want the skin of a ninety year old when you're only forty.

Thousands leave Florida every year blaming the six to nine months of heat and humidity as one of the reasons. Even when warned about it ahead of time, these buyers moved to Florida anyway because they didn't believe it was a big deal. Why? I've learned that Florida weather is one of those things that many have to actually experience to understand, and all calendars show summer lasting only three months each year.

One reason people don't believe the weather is that different from where they are moving is they have vacationed here during the summer for a week, and they survived. Even standing in long lines at a theme park to get on a ride, it didn't seem so bad. That's because you were distracted from the heat by the newness and excitement of the park. That's vacation. Now go to that same park everyday for 30 days straight in the summer and see if you notice any changes. I'd be willing to bet that every additional day you would be a little less thrilled by the rides and a lot more aware of the brutal heat, humidity, and the long lines. That's living here.

I've experienced years where it seemed like the humidity lasted the entire year. Florida is much closer to the equator than back home. The sun is much stronger during the traditional summer months as it is all year long. As a resident, you learn to avoid any direct exposure to it except maybe during the winter. Failure to do so will quickly ensure premature aging of the skin, possibly worse. That is why dermatologists and surgeons that cut cancer from the skin do a brisk business in Florida.

A family formerly from Ohio that wanted to move back called me to list their home. They complained about the weather among other things. "In Ohio, it gets hot, it gets humid, but not for 9 months straight without a break," he told me.

Hot days with high humidity in the north that happen occasionally can't prepare you for long summers in Florida. Hot days with high humidity week after week start to take their toll after four or five months or longer. This is one reason why there are just as many moving vans loaded with prized possessions heading north on I-95 and I-75 as heading south.

Recess is Supposed to be Fun

Shortly after I sold a home to a young family new to the state, I saw their name in the newspaper. Their son had a heat stroke while outdoors at school on lunch recess. It was only the beginning of May, but it already felt like the middle of summer by up north standards. I called them and was told that he was fine, but it was very scary for them. They said nothing like that had ever happened to him before. They were surprised by the incident and are now more concerned about the heat. They were afraid it could happen again but not with the same positive outcome.

The newspaper took the incident as an opportunity to caution and inform. Heat stroke is common in Florida and can happen to people of all ages. Many seemingly normal activities can put you in danger here, where back north you never had to think about it. People die from this every year. People in their mid-sixties and older must be especially careful because their bodies can't adjust to temperature as easily or quickly as when they were younger. Certain medications can also make it even harder for the body to regulate temperature. You may want to check with your doctor about medications you're taking before considering a move to a hotter climate.

A Different Golf Stroke

For most of the US, summer is prime time for golf, and most courses are closed in the winter. Not so in Florida. Winter is prime time, and that is when you will be charged the highest rates. Most courses cut their rates dramatically in April or May. From May through September you can expect to pay half price or less depending upon the day. Heat and humidity are the reason.

Summer discounts get larger as the sun gets stronger

and the heat index rises. You can play almost anywhere after two in the afternoon for half or less than the regular rate. You can get 18 holes in easily because nobody else will be out there to hold you up and it stays light until 9:30 pm.

I've had many different golf buddies in Florida throughout the years, but none that played consistently. A contractor friend of mine loved golf but stopped playing because it got too crowded in the winter and he couldn't take the heat in the summer.

Another friend in real estate first got into golf in his fifties and loved it. The only thing he loved more than golf was saving money. He always complained about the humidity but still would only play after two in the afternoon to get the lowest possible green fee. One outing around the twelfth hole I noticed he wasn't saying much. He looked pale. He said he didn't feel well but wanted to continue. When we got out of the cart to hit his next shot, he stumbled and fell. I helped him into the cart and rushed him back to the clubhouse. I was afraid he was having a heart attack. He got the attention he needed. It wasn't a heart attack, it was a heat stroke. He never played again.

The Sun on Steroids

Many a new Floridians have given in to the temptation to trade their trusty up north car or truck for a convertible. Between spring and fall up north, you'll probably have more days to enjoy a ride with the top down than you will in Florida all year. Winter in Florida is definitively convertible weather. The rest of the year is too hot and humid to enjoy it and there are occasional swarms of various bugs and violent thunder showers that can roll in quickly. The biggest concern is the sun.

Most weather reports in Florida will report the UV index. This index tells you how long you can be exposed to the sun before your skin begins to burn. Many days it is less than five minutes. I've met many long term Floridians whose face and arms are leather-like from working outside, years of driving a convertible or too many trips to the beach. The stronger sun causes damage quicker.

Air conditioned car to air conditioned home

Many soon-to-be Floridians say, "I'll just go from my air conditioned home to the air conditioned store and back, no big deal." That's true, as air conditioning is everywhere in modern Florida, but you can escape the cold up north by going from your heated home to your heated car. Living like this keeps you indoors though, so does it really matter where you are if you're indoors all the time? The difference is you only dodge the cold up north for three months a year, but the humidity in Florida lasts for 7-9 months. But here's a list of scenarios you may want to picture yourself in. In Florida, summer begins long before the calendar says so, and it lasts far past when the calendar says fall begins. You may experience this up to nine months a year:

As soon as you walk outside, the thick humidity smacks you in the face, and you instantly feel sweaty and uncomfortable, like you need to shower.

After being in a store for only a few minutes, you return to your car to find it is already 160 degrees inside. Do you stand outside in 90 degree 95% humidity and wait for the A/C to cool the car down or do you get in, stick to the seat and tolerate the 150 degree heat?

You park your car in the garage (everybody here that has one has an auto garage door opener). A half an hour later, you go into the garage and it's now 120 degrees in there because of the heat from the car's engine. Sweat some more.

You spent a fortune on outdoor furniture to eat and relax outside and enjoy the Florida lifestyle like the people in the brochures. In reality, it's too hot and humid to comfortably enjoy a meal outdoors most of the year, unless you like the taste of extra salt you get from sweat dripping into your food.

You paid a lot of extra money for a pool, only to learn that the water heats up to a warm bath of ninety degrees for many months. That doesn't offer much relief.

Köppen-Geiger Climate Zones of Florida

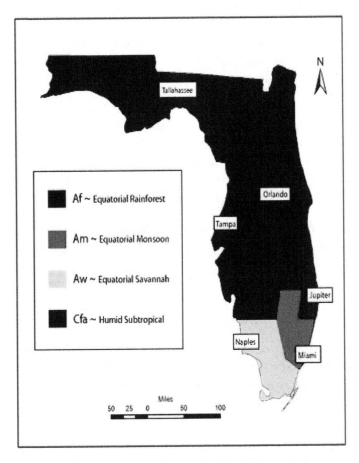

Elizabeth Donelan
University of South Florida
March 25, 2012

Source: Kottek et al. World Map of the Köppen-Geiger Climate Classification Updated. *Meteorologische Zeitschrift*, 15 (3), 2006. Projection: Robinson Compromise

I have met Floridians that seem to be immune to the muggy weather. I recall one particular listing appointment where I noticed that the windows were open in the middle of the afternoon on a hot humid day in August as I pulled in the driveway. As I walked into the home, I noticed a strong musty smell that can happen when too much moisture is allowed to get into the home and mold grows. As we sat at the kitchen table, they said one of the things they loved about their home was that it was situated in a way that provided a constant breeze, and there was no need to turn on the AC. As I sat there with this hot, humid air blowing over me, I started to sweat profusely. I felt like I was melting. This couple, probably in their 70s, sat there perfectly comfortable without a hint of perspiration. Remember, many people who move to Florida intending it to be a permanent one will end up moving out. Humidity is a main cause. Read about the different living options in later chapters. If you will be living in Florida full time, consider testing that choice by getting a seasonal rental after the snowbirds go home. Rent from April 1st through October if you can to get a better idea of what you are getting into every year. Surviving one year of the weather doesn't mean you're in the clear because for many it gets harder to take every, but at least you'll have a better idea of what it's like.

Location Considerations and Other Options

Choosing to live in north Florida can offer some relief because hot, humid, summer-like conditions won't last as long in Jacksonville as they would in Miami. You can't escape the humid climate anywhere in Florida though, as you can see from the map above. Since the climate zones in Florida don't exist in the northern US, it's understandable that many people don't realize how different living in Florida really is until they actually live there.

Just as "snowbirds" (northerners who go to Florida for a month or longer to escape the winter) flee the cold and head south, if you are a full time Florida resident, you could escape the summer for a cooler mountain town for a month or more every year. This can be far more affordable than you imagine. It could be just the break you need to prevent extra long Florida summers from becoming a dream buster. The quiet beach town I lived in when I first moved to Florida nearly shut down for the first few years during August. Real Estate brokers would close their offices, even restaurants closed because the owners left for cooler weather, often to New England or Canada.

Another excellent option is to own two affordable homes, one in Florida and the other in a cool mountain town, instead of one expensive home. This option will be discussed later in more detail because this is exactly how some of the happiest Florida residents I've met have arranged their life. If you aren't in Florida from June through October, you will escape almost all of the negatives that cause people to move out, including heat, humidity and hurricanes, etc.

Heat Stroke Awareness

Heat stroke symptoms: headache, muscle cramps, fatigue, dizziness, hot dry skin, flushed skin, high body temperature, unable to sweat, rapid pulse, rapid breathing, disorientation, seizures, loss of consciousness

Heat stroke complications: unconsciousness, shock, coma, permanent brain damage, death

"Complications of Heatstroke". Wednesday, January 26, 2011 8:13:00AM. April 11, 2011.
http://www.wrongdiagnosis.com/h/heatstroke/complic.htm

4. Ride the Money Roller Coaster

The Florida Economy can Improve or Deteriorate Quicker

Money problems, mainly not having enough of it, were another common theme cited for needing to move back north. Some people would just come out and tell me everything even though I didn't ask. Others would blame something else, but you could tell they were experiencing financial stress. The fickle see-saw economy of Florida can negatively affect retirees on a fixed budget as well as those who still need to work for income. Changes in the economy, increasing taxes, fast rising insurance rates and other financial matters that seem to happen overnight were singled out the most.

The cost of living in the state of Florida in the past

decades has traditionally been lower than most other states. You could move to Florida from just about anywhere else in the US and buy a home comparable to the one you left for a lot less money. Taxes were lower. Insurance was reasonable. The wages paid in Florida were lower, but so was the overall cost of living. That's one reason so many people moved to the state when they retired. Their money, social security and pensions could buy them a very comfortable retirement, often better than where they had moved from.

Starting in the early 2000s, that started to change. Real estate values started to climb higher than ever before. Higher property value led to higher real estate taxes. The record hurricane years of 2004 and 2005 led to vastly higher homeowners rates. The state that promised retirees warm weather and a low cost of living in the past changed, probably forever.

The state's economy has historically experienced frequent booms and busts. Before the "great recession" of 2008, Florida had nearly the lowest unemployment in the country and real estate prices were climbing the fastest. After the bust in 2008, Florida's housing values dropped an average of 60% ($200,000 house at $80,000?) and the state experienced the highest foreclosure rate in the US. Unemployment was among the worst in the country. When times get tough in Iowa, people just hunker down and ride it out. In Florida, tough times just gives people one more reason to move back home, which makes the economy here even worse.

During good economies, Florida has a lot of people moving to the state, causing growth and a hot real estate market. When that growth slows or stops, the bubble bursts. A lot of money can be made playing these booms and busts (a whole other book) but it presents problems for seniors on a fixed income and younger couples working for lower Florida wages while supporting a growing family. If moving down when the economy is in recession, home prices, rents and taxes may be low. That can change quickly when the economy heats up and causes real estate taxes, rent, insurance and others costs to rise.

Scrambled Nest Eggs

If you bought during a boom and are now selling into a common Florida bust, you will leave your nest egg here. I've seen it happen a lot. Some who became victims of a bad Florida economy have had to borrow money just to get out of the state.

Rarely have retired Floridians given employment as a reason for deciding to leave the state. Many do work just to get out of the house but some must go back to work because their cost of living went up. I have noticed an increase of seniors who say they must now work to make ends meet.

If you are flexible on hours, wages and benefits, you may find work, particularly part time. Pay in Florida in usually low when compared to most other states. Some blame retirees who will work for the low wages. Restaurants need cooks and waitresses, grocery stores need cashiers and baggers. Yes baggers. In a state with a higher percentage of senior citizens than most, many grocery stores still have baggers who will also insist on pushing the cart to your car and placing the bags in your car for you.

Full time employment with health benefits and a higher wage that can support a growing young family can be hard to come by. Health care, of course, is an exception because of the large percentage of older citizens. If you work in this field, you can be hired quickly with higher pay even before you move to the state.

Construction is another area that can provide higher wages and plenty of work, but that depends on what phase Florida's economy is in, boom or bust, and what real estate market you are in. If a hurricane has caused millions or billions of dollars in damages to an area, you can find work at a great pay rate because all that damage has to be repaired or replaced. Since there will be insurance dollars to pay for it, that will lift an area's economy like a giant bubble. When the insurance repair bubble bursts, there will be layoffs.

If you are moving to an area that is experiencing explosive growth because of retirees flocking to the place, you can get hired just by showing up. I have seen new construction so hot that contractors would drive around and try to hire people right off other contractors' job sites.

If you were looking for work in construction after a bust, forget it. In Florida, the booms are hotter and the busts are the worst you'll find anywhere. When it's hot, everybody is making money and anybody who moves to Florida can find a job. When it all stops, the opposite is true. Smaller builders who were supposed to warrant repairs on new homes go broke or leave town. Pawn shops fill with tools of the construction trades to the point where they won't take anymore.

Starting or Buying a Business

It didn't take me long to notice something quite different about Florida compared to the state I came from. When selling real estate, buyers have to give you basic income and asset information so you can determine what they can afford. Overall, the wages that workers earned in Florida were lower than in other states for the same occupations. The owners of small businesses, however, made more than they probably would in another state.

During boom times, new residents pour into the state. This can happen very quickly. I watched the population explode in my area and not a single new business opened for awhile. This meant long lines at restaurants to sit down for a meal or being 10 cars back at the drive through. Want a new home built when the economy is hot in FL? Can you wait a year or a year and a half? Fast growth provides lots of extra cash for the small business owners because more customers must spend their money with you because there are no new competitors.

Beware though, because the boom times are usually quickly followed by a bust. I had a customer who was a general contractor. After a hurricane came through a nearby area, his business took off. He signed millions in contracts to repair the damage. More workers had to be brought in from other states to handle all the work.

Unemployment was unheard of. Builders were throwing up new homes like crazy. Because these new workers were working 7 days a week and making a lot of cash, the stores and restaurants were filled. Buyers would walk into a model home, but if the builder didn't have something they could move into right away, the buyer would walk right out because many people had just sold their home up north and needed a place to move into in thirty days. That's why builders put up spec homes all over the place. They would borrow a bunch of money and put up a bunch of homes so when people demanded a finished new home, the builder would have one to sell them.

I got a call from an old customer who was a contractor about a worker of his who wanted to buy a new home. This young kid had moved to Florida from Michigan with his girlfriend. He was working 7 days a week and had saved enough money for a down payment on a home. They bought a brand new three bedroom, two bath, two car garage home through me for $214,000 near the height of a boom that lasted for about 2 ½ years. After the millions in insurance for hurricane rebuilding ran out, the contractors started laying workers off. This young new homeowner was let go.

Real estate values started to sink. This was simple

supply and demand. All the newly unemployed families needed to sell and move, but nobody was buying. Everybody was selling. The young guy from Michigan didn't even try to sell, because the value of his home dropped so fast. He ended up owing far more on his mortgage than the home was worth. At one point his home was decreasing in value about $5000 a month. After he moved back to Michigan, his foreclosed home came on the market for $115,000, $100,000 less than he bought for it for just two years prior. After working mostly seven days a week for years, this guy and his small family left the state with nothing.

Florida was one of the states that the 2008 housing bust started in. The hardest hit areas were the ones that had few employers other than construction and tourism related businesses.

When the building stopped, thousands of workers became unemployed. These unemployed workers stopped spending money. Restaurants, tire stores and builders started to fail and close. Where I was living at the time, my favorite wine and beer shop closed. I knew they were in trouble when they shut down the coolers and only sold room temperature beer.

Banks started to foreclose on these unsold new homes. Many homeowners lost a lot of money. Buyers who came down and paid $250,000 cash for a home now had a home worth maybe half that, if you could find a buyer at all. Buyers who put a lot of money down and got a mortgage to buy saw that equity disappear as the value dropped below what they owed. For a lot of those folks, that was their whole nest egg.

One customer of mine who was a contractor didn't fare any better. After working hard for years and putting lots of money out for labor and materials on hundreds of new spec homes, the builders he contacted with couldn't sell those homes and went bust. They owed him hundreds of thousands of dollars, but couldn't pay. His business closed. He was forced to get a job far from his home and commuted home to his wife and family on weekends. He spent the little free time he had to file lawsuits and liens to try to get paid for the work he did, but often there's nothing left to go after.

Moving to Florida and starting a new business may be a great income idea and provide a much needed service to the community. You just need to look at the area closely and, most importantly, find out where in the boom and bust cycle that area is in at the moment. That isn't as hard to do as it sounds. You can start right from where you live now. Pick an area and call five real estate agents. If only one gets back to you, times are good. If you call five and speak to all of them right away, that could signal a lean period.

Big Money in Grab Bars Business

Finding a need and satisfying it can put a lot of cash in a business person's pocket. In most of Florida, that means serving seniors. I worked with a couple looking for a luxurious waterfront pool home with access to the Gulf of Mexico. They loved to fish, and the home they were looking for had to have a dock in the back for the new boat they just bought. They were doing very well.

They were willing to pay cash and were looking for a good deal. They had their own small business for years. What did they do? Grab bars. Just grab bars and nothing else. Having a grab bar in the shower and other areas for safety and convenience was apparently something many seniors desired. They were the grab bar kings for all the surrounding counties. They had a small crew that installed lots of them every day. I had no idea there was so much money in something like that.

A word of caution to prospective entrepreneurs. In the past, many fly by night operators took advantage of senior citizens in Florida. They sold home sites where you couldn't build a home. They did shoddy home repair work. Many took money down for repair work and left town. To prevent this from happening today, state licenses and permits are usually required for almost everything and they aren't easy to get. Just because you ran a roofing company up north, doesn't necessarily mean you can just start one in Florida. You will probably have to do a lot more to start doing business in Florida, including becoming certified by the state. Certified experience, notarized statements, bonding, workman's comp and more. This could have something to do with the lack of competing businesses and higher profits for small business owners that are able to open for business. Investigate all licensing requirements on the state and local level thoroughly before investing.

Being aware of where Florida's economy is in the boom and bust cycle (it can very different than the US as a whole) can be very important because the studies show there is a realistic possibility that a permanent move to Florida will not work out. If you move to Florida when the economy is great and buy when home prices are high, you can lose a lot of money if you must sell during a bust and prices have collapsed. If you buy (steal) a home in Florida during a bust when prices are low, selling at a higher price and making a profit makes a decision to move out of the state much easier. Be careful though, as asking a real estate agent or a builder if it's a good time to buy may yield inaccurate advice. I have never met one who didn't think that "now" was a good time to buy.

Florida's boom periods usually last much longer than the bust times, the 2008 bust not included. Prepare during these prolonged good times to survive the inevitable bust periods. Florida's economy can be hot for many years. The bust periods can be brutal and happen quickly (oil spill, red tide, etc.) but it's usually not very long before things improve, so those who prepare to survive the dips can thrive when things get better.

Florida's real estate prices can increase higher and quicker than states with slow or stable population growth, which will cause taxes to rise quickly due to increased assessments that are adjusted yearly. Homeowners insurance rates can jump after a bad hurricane season and make a home cost more than those on a fixed income can afford. Natural and manmade disasters can affect Florida's economy and therefore employment more so than the state you are moving from. Those with fixed incomes or lower incomes that depend on industries that can be affected by disasters should plan accordingly to avoid being forced to leave the state because of financial difficulties. From Wiki: In 2009, the US Census Bureau estimated that Floridians spent an average 49.1% of personal income on housing-related costs, the third highest percentage in the country.

Interesting Economic Facts

Florida's per person income growth rate dropped to 45th in the US in 2009.

More Floridians are living in poverty in 2009 than 2008 and more than 10% of residents lived on food stamps.

The rate of growth of the total value of Florida's goods and services slowed from 2006 to 2009, making the state rank 47th in the US.

Population growth is what has fueled Florida's economy in the past. That growth has slowed to near zero, and some projections show it won't return to its historic growth for at least 20 years.

"Troubling Trends Threaten Florida's Well Being". Florida Center For Fiscal And Economic Policy. Annual Economic Review July 2009. www.aboutpinellaskids.org

5. Environmental Downgrading

The Beaches and Fishing

One of the reasons you may be considering Florida is its natural beauty. The tropical-like climate produces lush scenery, including the famous palm tree. You can easily grow oranges and grapefruit in your back yard in much of the state. The place is filled with many variations of birds and other wildlife. What you probably don't know from vacations here is the full effect growth and other factors have had on this beauty. No, I am not a tree hugging environmentalist, but no long time Floridian can ignore the environmental changes that have taken place.

For the first few years I lived in Florida I loved the beach. I was on the west coast and lived about 6 minutes from a quiet little beach village on a narrow key. The beach was very clean, people were sparse, and the water was warm and clear most of the year. It was just like in the travel brochures. Postcard perfect. That didn't last.

First came the road expansion. The sleepy two lane main road on the mainland just off the key was expanded to four to six lanes with a higher speed limit. At first this did not bother me at all. I was in the business of selling homes. More lanes would bring more people. More people meant more homes would need be built, which meant more sales and money. The larger road brought more traffic and people almost immediately. The sleepy subdivisions were soon noisy little boom areas with trucks of all types flying around as ground everywhere was being torn up to build new homes.

The small peaceful beach village started to change too. The "old Florida" mom and pop businesses were being bought and torn down to make way for new high rise condos on the beach. Cozy 10 unit old Florida "tiki" beach motels with character were replaced by sixty units of cold concrete structure surrounded by macadam. That often included a large loss of natural Florida vegetation that surrounded the quaint old Florida buildings, replaced with parking lots. Hundreds of palm trees and other vegetation that were home to lots of interesting wildlife were destroyed, replaced by a few token palms at the entrance.

Even More Macadam

Because there were now more people going to the same size beach, the old beach parking lots began to fill up. If you drove to the beach, you were not guaranteed to be able to use it because there may not be a place for you to park. Of course, they solved this problem by putting in larger parking lots. Because the old lots were surrounded by roads and condos, the only place they could expand the macadam was towards the water. This meant more macadam, cars, and people, but less beach. To pay for this, the parking fees went up. Before, you could pay one low fee for the entire day, but you now pay by the hour. You now pay more to go to less beach.

I enjoy the beach less when it's hard to walk to the water without stepping on someone and there's more litter and cigarette butts in the sand and floating in the water. As more people move to Florida, I don't see this improving. You can't make more beach, and, in fact, many existing beaches are shrinking from erosion.

More Beach Closings

In all the years that I vacationed in Florida prior to moving here, I never experienced a beach that was closed. The same was true for the first few years of living here as a full-time resident, and I went to the beach regularly. As the population grew, beach cautions and closings, mostly due to high bacteria count from fecal matter (What? Yuck!) started. Some blamed it on the area's growth and some said it was because the authorities were testing the water more often.

Beach cautions and closings in Florida are now likely to decrease due to budget problems at all levels of government. In 2011, the State of Florida ceased all funding for the testing of water off Florida's beaches. Now some beaches may not be tested and others tested every two weeks instead of weekly as in the past. Less testing means more people will likely get sick after swimming at Florida's beaches.

More Homes Means More Pesticides and Weed Killers

When you shop for a home in Florida, you can't help but notice all the picture perfect lawns. Lush green grass, perfectly trimmed bushes and not a weed in site. If you go to a condo complex or visit a golf course, everything looks so neat and manicured. You'll notice little or no weeds or bugs, both of which the real Florida are loaded with. What happened to all the weeds and bugs?

Navigating your car down a quiet residential street in the morning here provides a clue. You will see a small army of trucks and trailers parked all over the road. They are the workers who cut the grass, spray the lawns for weeds and apply fertilizer. Others spray pesticides for bugs. Picture perfect weed-free, bug-less lawns don't just happen on their own. They get that way by constantly applying massive amounts of pesticides, weed killer and fertilizer much of which contains toxic chemicals. They wear masks while spraying the stuff and post warning signs in the yard.

The problem with this is that heavy Florida downpours wash that stuff into the very water that you swim and fish in. I used to prefer buying and enjoying locally harvested seafood when I first moved to Florida when the area was more natural and pristine. I don't anymore.

What is Red Tide

For the first five years I lived in Florida during the '90s, I enjoyed the local beaches without interruption. Then came the first episode of red tide. The scientists still don't know everything about this toxic algae bloom, but they believe it feeds off of the fertilizer and other runoff that gets washed into the water. Once the chemicals are washed into the warm water and heated by the strong Florida sun, the bloom explodes.

What the authorities do know is the bloom takes all of the oxygen out of the water and kills all the fish, crabs, and whatever else that used to live in the water. The first time it happened, I went to the beach to see for myself. What I saw was sickening.

Dead rotting fish rolling in the surf, rotting carcasses all along the beaches, as far as I could see in both directions. The smell made me want to vomit. This algae releases toxins into the air, and the wind can carry it inland for miles, causing respiratory problems in some people. I started to gag from the smell and had to leave. I did not go fishing or eat local seafood in a restaurant since that sight. Years later, I still remember that vividly.

That was not the only outbreak. It became almost common, just like hurricanes some years were worse than others. If the experts are correct and the fertilizer used on lawns and in agriculture of which Florida is a leader, as more people move, the red tide outbreaks will increase.

There was a Canadian couple who rented a beautiful pool home across the street from me every winter. He was a lawyer with a successful practice that allowed him and his wife to come down every February for a break from the cold Canadian winter. They had been doing this for over a decade.

One year we had a red tide outbreak that was particularly bad. It started in the summer and lasted into the winter in varying strengths. This Canadian couple looked forward to going to the beach to soak up some warm rays, go for a swim, and do a little fishing. If they didn't catch anything, they had a favorite little beachfront restaurant they would visit. They usually went to the beach almost every day when they were here, but red tide changed all that. The wife got sick the first day they were there from the smell. Red tide was present for the entire month they were here. They were so disgusted they swore they would never come back. The following year the home sat empty during February.

As a businessman in Florida, I first welcomed the growth spurts. More development means more money. But the more they rip up old Florida to replace it with more macadam and larger, taller look-alike concrete buildings, the more I sensed a loss. Quaint historic buildings with character were being replaced with cookie cutter buildings, massive parking lots and malls. Every year there were fewer unique mom and pop restaurants and shops, and more Burger Kings, Taco Bells, and Walmarts.

From what I've seen, every year Florida looks more like Detroit, Cleveland or any other place. More people, parking lots, litter, franchises and less fish, pelicans and dolphins. Left unchecked, the very things that attract people to the state could be destroyed. Then people won't come here anymore. Maybe that's what is already happening.

Red Tide

Fish kill washing up on beach

Moving to Florida for the Beach

If you are moving to Florida because you love fishing, swimming, boating or other recreations that would involve the beaches and water surrounding Florida, it would be wise to research the water quality first. Check the history of beaches being closed due to red tide, high bacteria counts and other occurrences of the area you are considering. Some beaches have consistently more problems than others.

In general, the water off the west coast of Florida in The Gulf of Mexico is clearer, warmer and the waves are gentler. That doesn't mean the water quality is better than the cooler, darker water of the Atlantic Ocean off of Florida's east coast. The Gulf of Mexico is "refreshed" less by water from other bodies of water because it is almost totally sealed off by land, where the Atlantic waters are not. There is also a growing "dead zone" in the Gulf of Mexico that is thousands of square miles in size.

Another thing to be aware of is Cuba is drilling for oil not far off the coast of Florida with an oil rig they purchased from China. The US prevents drilling for oil in the waters surrounding Florida to protect the beaches and tourism, but they couldn't stop Cuba from doing the same thing. It's been reported that water currents would send oil from a disaster in that area onto the beaches of Florida. Please be aware that risks to your enjoyment of Florida's beaches and property values of coastal areas appear to be increasing.

Information on Florida beach closings can be found at:

The National Resource Defense Council
http://www.nrdc.org/water/oceans/ttw/

US Environmental Protection Agency
http://water.epa.gov/type/oceb/beaches/beaches_ind ex.cfm

Information on red tide itself, as well as current and historical conditions can be found at the US National Oceanic and Atmospheric Administration.
http://tidesandcurrents.noaa.gov/hab/

Oiled bird on beach photo taken by "marinephotobank."

6. Water Fire and Crawlers

Drought and Drinking Water

Over the last several years the weather pattern in Florida, like most of the country, seems to be getting more unpredictable. Florida traditionally has a rainy season that begins in June and ends in September. During the summer in the past, you could count on the days being mostly sunny, but at some point every afternoon the sky would turn black and you would get a brief downpour. The sun would then come back out and dry things up quickly. It doesn't always happen like that anymore.

In recent times, Florida has suffered drought conditions in many areas more often. This has affected the amount of drinking water available. Many homes with well water have seen them go dry due to a lack of rain. This is something to keep in mind when shopping for a home because what do you do with a home if your well runs dry and you can't hook up to central water and sewer?

If you have municipal water you may also suffer. In order to conserve water, many municipalities have changed their rates to punish people they feel are using too much. One of the counties I lived in took water from a river to process into drinking water. Twice they asked for a waiver from the U.S. so they could take water closer to the river bottom muck than is normally allowed. They also wanted to put more chlorine in the water than the standards normally allowed in order to treat it. They claimed the water was the same and safe to drink, but it looked and smelled different to me so I would not use it for drinking water after that.

Water, or the lack of it, is a serious issue in Florida. Up north I was billed for water quarterly, and considered the bill a nuisance because I had to pay a bill for such a small amount. When I moved into my first home in Florida, I cleaned everything inside and out, washed the car and topped off the pool. My first water bill for the month was over a hundred and fifty dollars. For a month! I called the water company to have the obviously incorrect bill straightened out. Instead, I was the one that got straightened out. Water was going to cost me much more now that I moved to Florida and there wasn't anything I could do about it except conserve. If you live on a fixed income or on a tight budget, get the facts on the cost of water and sewer service for the home you want to buy before you sign the offer.

Thirsty Lawns

If you buy a home in Florida that does not have a sprinkler system, your lawn will most likely die off over time. It will also become brown and brittle during the winter because rain is rare in most of Florida in the winter months.

If you have a sprinkler system, you can keep your lawn green and lush, but it will also grow faster so you will have to cut it more often or pay to have someone do it. A sprinkler can also come with some unwanted responsibilities during droughts. Some municipalities limit the use of sprinkler systems to only certain times of specific days to conserve water. They do change the allowed days and times and you must keep up with their program or you could face a fine.

Many homes with central water have a separate well just for the sprinkler system. With this "yard well," the water is free. Wells are a lot less expensive to put in than up north because the water is closer to the surface. A sprinkler hooked up to the central water source can cost you a small fortune compared to the free water that is supplied by a yard well.

A drought in my area got so bad that you were only allowed to water early in the morning, one day a week. They also gave every county employee the power to write tickets for fines if you didn't comply. Imagine, a county janitor in the neighborhood that can slap you with a $500 fine for over-watering your yard.

Florida is the also the lightning capital of the world. Blackouts, brownouts and power surges are common and can throw off the timer on your sprinkler system. That can make you an unintentional lawbreaker if you aren't there to catch it.

Boating is More Fun With Water

Have a boat or always wanted one? If you plan on buying a waterfront home with access to the gulf or ocean, make sure you get all the facts on the waterway leading from your home out to the main bodies of water you want to enjoy. Waterfront property with boating access is highly desirable and therefore some of the highest priced real estate available. You will not only pay much more to purchase waterfront with access, but you will pay more in taxes every year on the higher value.

I have worked with many couples just moving down that have conflicting desires regarding a boat and waterfront homes. The issue is the huge difference in the type of home you can get for the same money, waterfront (with access to large water) compared to non-waterfront.

If you have $250,000, you may be able to get a large, newer home with many baths and bedrooms, a family room, high ceilings, granite counter tops, heated spa that spills into a caged pool and more, located on a non-waterfront standard lot in a good location. For the same money, you may only get a smaller, older home with an obsolete floor plan, two bedrooms, one bath, on a well located waterfront lot. Usually it's clear to the wife if she's not a boater; she wants the big, comfortable new home. He wants the waterfront house and a boat. Unless you have been avid boaters for years, the non-waterfront lot is usually the better choice. You will be happier in the nicer home, based upon feedback from many of my home buyers that faced this same choice, unless both spouses are already boating fanatics when they move to Florida.

I not only sold newcomers many waterfront homes, but I lived on a canal and saw what happens. New buyers from up north that never owned a boat before buy a costly waterfront home on a canal with access to major water and move in. They buy a boat to put in the backyard. They use it every day for the first couple of weeks. Then it's once or twice a month. After a year, the lonely boat just sits on the lift, unused and dropping in value. Finally, after years of not being used at all, just before it's completely worthless, they sell it. Do you know the two happiest days in a boater's life? The day he buys the boat and the day he sells it.

Did you know that Florida has experienced some of the worst drought conditions in its history recently? Many waterfront properties have canals that lead to a creek or river on the way to the ocean or gulf. If you are a new boater, make sure you learn what kind of boat and draft you will need to have before you spend the extra cash for the waterfront. Newbies have paid a fortune for a waterfront home only to learn they can't get their new cruiser out to the big water because although the water in the back of their home is deep, two blocks away from their home the water is too shallow for their new boat to get through. Or the boat you bought can't fit under one of the bridges between you and the Gulf.

Serious droughts in recent years have meant lower water levels in normally boat-able waterways that have prevented boating. There are also waterways that are only passable during high tide or during the summer when the river and creek levels are higher from the rainy season.

If you are buying a waterfront home for boating, make sure you get a real estate agent who is a waterfront specialist. I don't mean an agent that just advertises herself that way, but doesn't even own a boat. Only use a true waterfront specialist. This is an agent who lives on water themselves, has a boat and uses it regularly. It won't cost you a penny extra to work with an expert like this, but the advice will be priceless. The true waterfront specialist is an agent that can show you homes by taking you there in their boat, right to their home's own dock.

Another huge advantage of using a pro like this is that you can get free advice on the best type of boat to buy to enjoy the water in your area. Trust me, if you are new to boating or Florida, this is more complicated than you may think. You can get my expert help in finding the right agent to work with in Florida through a free service listed in the back of this book.

Orange Glow and Smoke Smell at Night

You may have visited the state many times without ever seeing or even hearing about a wildfire. Rain in Florida during the winter can be rare. While this contributes to near perfect weather, the sun is still strong and can dry out brush and lawns, causing a fire hazard. Fire season in Florida starts the same time hurricane season ends.

Just when you are safe from evacuations due to hurricanes, a wildfire may cause one. Like hurricanes, you can have years with little or no threat or years with severe drought and high threat. Where you live will also affect the possible threat. You don't have wildfires in downtown Miami, but you may in Cape Coral.

Wildfires can burn for days or weeks. One area I lived in, you could count on at least one big wildfire every year. Large clouds of smoke formed in the air and you could taste the smoke with every breath. When I first moved down, I drove towards the first one I saw. I ran into a police line blocking off the area. Lots of people were there to watch. I could see homes that were untouched by the fire, but all the trees and brush of the vacant lots around them were charred to a crisp. Boats, sheds, anything near the vacant lots were burnt too.

There was a large state park preserve near one of my homes where wildfires were common. The fire department tried starting controlled burns to cut down on the amount of available combustible brush.

87

At night you could see the large red and yellow glow of the fire not that far away. You could smell the smoldering ashes for days afterward. This alone did not affect most homeowners to the point of moving unless a fire got so close that the first responders had to hose down their home to keep the fire away.

It is just something you should be aware of if you are going to be shopping for a new home. You may have trouble sleeping while smelling smoke and seeing the glow of a large fire outside your window instead of the normal dark of night. These fires only occasionally make it into a neighborhood filled with homes, thanks to the fire crews. If you were close to buying in a certain neighborhood and wanted to know about the wildfire danger, I would contact the closest fire department rather than ask the real estate agent or owner of the home. If you're torn between choosing from two homes you like, finding out the wildfire risk may help you decide.

Flooding

Shortly after I first moved to Florida, my area experienced a tropical storm-like event, but the winds never increased to the point where it became a named tropical storm. It just started to rain one day and continued to rain for five days straight. It rained day and night without stopping. I had never seen anything like it before. Like many newer homes, my home sat quite a bit higher than the road. There was a grass greenbelt swale (man-made depression) behind my home to drain storm water to canals that eventually led to the Gulf. During this storm, I watched as the water slowly started to fill the road in front of my home and the swale behind it, making my home an island. As the days went by, the water slowly rose toward my home. We were advised by the authorities to stay inside if it was dry or go to a shelter if our home was flooding. How we were supposed to get to the shelter, I didn't know. The water that filled the street was so high, I wouldn't want to risk driving through it.

When the rain finally stopped and the water level slowly lowered on the street to just a couple of inches, I went out for a drive in it. I drove around my newer community and a nearby one where the homes were older. They were built before building codes mandated homes be built a certain height above the level of the road. These people in the older homes were already putting piles of carpet, furniture and other flood damaged belongings out for the trash collectors. That's why some older homes may be cheaper to buy but far more costly to insure and own.

The strange thing about the storm was that there was no real advance warning from the weather forecasters or authorities ahead of time. It was just supposed to be a few days of mostly rain that happened to turn into heavy rain for five straight days. That was one of the first "welcome to Florida, it's different here" events that I never thought of or learned about in my research before moving to the Sunshine State.

Snakes, Alligators & Bugs

The state you're living in probably has at least some of these creatures. Florida just has a lot more of them. When I lived up north, I may have encountered a snake every couple of years. That includes jogging, biking and hiking on trails through the woods and mountains. When I moved to Florida, my encounters increased dramatically.

Snakes in Florida

Snakes, like gators, are more active when it's warmer. They also like to eat geckos, the kind that don't have a British accent and hock insurance in commercials for a paycheck from Geico. Geckos are abundant, fast, nervous lizard-like little creatures. The ones in Florida are too busy running for their lives to save you any money on car insurance. They are faster than the bugs they eat but not always faster than the snakes that like to eat them.

I once encountered five snakes in less than 45 minutes while jogging along a bike trail one sunny summer afternoon. Four of them just slithered quickly across the trails macadam in front of me. One that was very thick, about 5 foot long with a rattle at the end, just stopped and laid almost end to end the width of the trail. So I stopped about 30 feet from it. I wasn't about to try to go around or over it. So I just waited. After a few minutes, it slowly moved away and disappeared into the tall grass on the side if the trail. If you love to explore the outdoors but are terrified of snakes, you may want to give moving to Florida more serious thought.

Alligators Eat Pets and People

You are more likely to encounter alligators the farther south in Florida you live. Do you have a little dog that is like part of the family? Then you may want to consider the cooler northern part for Fido's sake or avoid waterfront properties in south Florida. Every time a pet is eaten by an alligator it makes the headlines in Florida. Apparently "gator eats pet" stories sell a lot of papers.

After living in the southern half of Florida for many years, I realized that any canal, lake, pond, large puddle or drainage pipe could be home to an alligator, if even for a short time. I have seen golfers on a green near a lake putting calmly, not realizing that an eight foot alligator is sunning himself just a short distance away. When I was still new to the state and looking for a golf ball, I nearly walked right up to what I thought was just a small log floating near where my ball went. A golf buddy yelled, warning me that it was a gator. Its body and most of its massive head was hidden below the surface of the dark water. In Florida you learn that something floating in the water could have a big mouth with sharp teeth, and after you see enough of them, you can usually distinguish a gator's head from a log or debris floating in the water.

Occasionally there will be reports of someone being killed by an alligator. Like pet deaths, these events get a lot of attention in the media. Often the victim was engaging in an activity that probably wasn't such a smart idea, like going for a swim in a lake that is known to have alligators. Other victims were new to Florida and didn't understand the risk.

Gators prefer to travel at night, sometimes traveling over land to go from one water source to another. Occasionally people wake up to find a gator in their pool. Reporters love to cover these stories too, especially if they get video of authorities removing the beast. I must admit, it is interesting watching people trying to get a big angry gator out of a pool and into a vehicle. The gator never seems to want to cooperate, and it never goes as smoothly as planned. I always do a gator check before going in the pool, especially at night, even though I've never had a problem in all the years I've lived in Florida.

An alligator swimming with an adult deer in its jaws.

Bugs, Bugs, Bugs

Do you know what a fire ant hill looks like? If you don't, that's OK, because you will learn. Fire ant hills are usually very small and hard to notice. That is until you encounter one the first time. Fire ants will swarm and start biting before you realize what is happening. Every bite stings and could last for hours. Learning what these mini monsters' homes look like can save you from a painful experience.

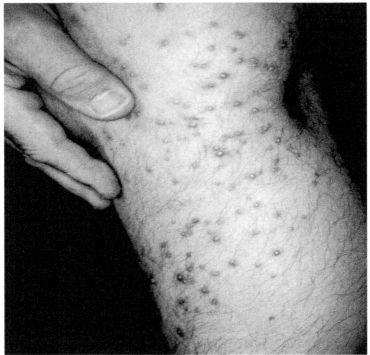

Fire ant bites three days later

More Mosquitoes and Termites

If your lanai or pool isn't screened, Mosquitoes can prevent you from enjoying the outdoors as often as you could otherwise. This is especially true the farther south in Florida you go. Dusk and dawn can bring roaming swarms of mosquitoes, gunning for your blood. Sure, you have mosquitoes where you live now but probably not nearly the same number of them. To enjoy living in Florida, you learn how to avoid them. Large screened outdoor areas like a lanai and screened pool cage make that easier.

Termites are also more of a problem here than most other states. You'll want to avoid any home that could be an easy meal for hungry termites. Termites are just about everywhere in Florida. That's fine, they have a their natural purpose. Just keep their home and your home separate, and you'll be fine.

Palmetto Bug or Giant Flying Cockroach

While looking at homes in Florida, particularity vacant properties, you may encounter a large flying insect that looks just like a giant cockroach. Before you get too grossed out, the salesperson will probably tell you that it's just a "palmetto bug." They probably wouldn't be lying to you because most people in Florida have been told this for decades, and it's now accepted as fact.

The palmetto is a plant common to much of Florida. Legend has it that a sharp Florida land salesperson from back in day, when they flew unsuspecting northerners in to sell them overpriced retirement lots (unbuildable swamp land), figured out that telling potential purchasers the giant cockroaches were just palmetto bugs sold more lots. The name stuck and, even today, most Florida residents, including real estate sales people, don't know these insects really are just what they look like, giant cockroaches.

The "palmetto bug" made its way from overseas to the southern US and loves warmth and humidity, of which Florida has an abundance of both. Unlike many of its roach relatives, the palmetto bug can grow up to two inches in length and will not scatter when you turn on a light. They don't look like they fly because their wings are hidden unless they're airborne. They don't fly around like a bird, but instead make quick low flights not far off the ground.

Palmetto bugs generally live outdoors but are commonly found inside homes seeking warmth from cooler weather. When they choose to call your home theirs, they will usually choose a moist area like the bathroom. They produce a fowl odor which can be left on surfaces they crawl across. They have been known to eat just about anything, including makeup, hair and beer. The drunk ones are easier to kill by stepping on them because they are slower. OK, that last one I don't know about for sure, it was just a guess.

In very rare cases, they have been known to bite humans when there is nothing else for them to eat. They are known to be bacteria carriers and can contaminate surfaces and cause illness in humans. They can also cause allergic skin reactions and asthma.

Spider or Wolf

I won't spend a lot of time on wolf spiders because they pose very little real risks to humans, but they may be larger than any spider you've ever seen in your home, so you should be aware of them before moving to Florida. Most wolf spiders are large, thick and hairy. They like to stay on the ground and don't spin webs. They are predators that mostly hunt at night and have great eyesight. They are often recognized by their two large forward looking eyes that sit on top of four smaller ones that may not be noticeable (if so, you may be too close). They can actually help keep harmful spiders away because they compete for territory, but most people kill these spiders or call an exterminator when they're found inside the home. They are common in most of Florida.

Other Buggers

During spring and summer, make sure your car has good wipers and plenty of windshield fluid when traveling Florida's interstates. Often you will have to use your wipers to clear "love-bugs" and other insects from your windshield. When driving in the summer (all six-plus months of it) large juicy insects splatting on your windshield and immediately being baked on by the powerful summer sun is routine. You'll get used to it. The car wash business is good in FL.

When you live in Florida, it will be hard to ignore many of these pests because they'll live closer to you than the Smiths next door. A seller never told me that any creature mentioned in this chapter was the main reason they were leaving Florida, but some were mentioned when people had a long list of things they disliked about the state. Prospective residents should just determine before moving if any of these things will really bug them (sorry I couldn't resist the pun).

Florida Alligator Facts

Florida alligators can grow to about 15 feet and weigh a half ton.

An alligator can run faster than a man in short bursts.

An alligator can swim faster than you can paddle a canoe.

An alligator can kill and eat smaller prey in one bite.

Alligators use a "death roll" to kill larger victims by taking them underwater and spinning violently.

Three women were killed in Florida by gators in separate attacks in a one week period in 2006.

Florida Snake Facts

There are 44 species of snakes in Florida, 6 are venomous.

"Pit-vipers" cause 99% of all snakebites in the US. All pit-vipers, like rattlesnakes and water moccasins, can be found in Florida.

Florida Bug Facts

There are so many kinds of bugs in Florida, they haven't all been cataloged yet. Over 150 new bug arrivals from overseas now consider themselves Floridians since 1986 alone.

7. Homeowners Insurance Traps

The Result of Record Hurricane Activity and Losses in 2004 and 2005

The cost to insure a property in Florida can be huge factor in why people move from this state. Insurance companies experienced enormous losses in property damage by record hurricane activity in 2004 and 2005. That caused the insurance companies to seek seemingly continual rate hikes to make up the losses and prepare for future storm outlays. Some companies will no longer insure homes in Florida because they consider the risk of loss to be too high. If you have been with the same company for years and planned on using them when you moved to Florida, check to see if they will write policies there. Allstate, Farmers, Geico, Progressive, State Farm and Travelers are just some of the companies that have been reported to have stopped issuing new policies in the past.

In 2004 I was notified by the insurance company that insured my homes for 10 years that they were not going to renew my policy. The reason? They were not renewing or writing any new policies in Florida. They were not going to do business in the state any longer.

I thought, no big deal, I'll just get another company. I called my insurance agent and was told that only two companies out of all the insurance companies in the world were writing new policies in my area. My home being 10 years old and so close to the Gulf of Mexico, however, did not qualify for either one of them. What? The only choice I had was the insurer of last resort, Citizens Insurance.

Citizens is an insurer set up by the State of Florida to serve as the homeowners insurance company for a last resort. If it wasn't for Citizens, many homes in Florida would have become uninsurable starting in 2004. My new cost was 300% more than I was paying. Nice. Almost $5,000 a year for homeowners and flood insurance with a higher deductible and less protection.

Having the state get involved in the business of homeowners insurance has solved a problem, namely preventing the economic disaster that would unfold if Florida homeowners suddenly were told they could not get insurance on their home at all. Mortgage companies and banks will not lend money on homes unless the home is protected by homeowners insurance. Insurance must be maintained on homes that already have a mortgage, or they would be in default and the lender could foreclose. There are many critics who say the state is risking a double disaster. They claim Citizens Insurance would not have enough funds to cover homeowners' losses when the next bad hurricane season happens because the lower rate they charge does not match the risk.

New Resident Shock

Most new buyers coming from other states are shocked when they attempt to secure homeowners insurance. After signing a contract to buy a home, they call the insurance company they've been with for decades, only to find their company doesn't insure homes in Florida. Or the company may have capped the number of policies in the state to limit their risk and can't write new insurance at that time.

Before large insurance companies can raise rates in Florida, they have to get approval from state regulators because every rate hike can create a financial hardship for citizens, especially those on a fixed income like retirees. This causes the state to turn rate increases down. The company then does not renew existing polices, write new policies or leaves the state altogether because they say they can't afford to take such a large risk for such low rates.

In any given area, insurance companies know about how many people will have a fender bender next month or how many 50 year old males will die from a heart attack. They know this because they have tons of stable data and therefore know what rates to charge. No one knows how many hurricanes will hit Florida two years from now and what the damage will cost to repair. It could be the worst ever and again break all records.

The unpredictability of the future cost of homeowners, flood, wind, sinkhole and other insurance to protect homes in Florida should be considered by everyone thinking of moving to Florida. I have seen homeowners insurance increases force people out of their homes in the past and see no reason why it wouldn't happen again. Residing inland in a newer home not in a high hazard flood, sinkhole or wind zone with the best storm protection is probably the best way to minimize the risk.

You Can't Get Insurance at All, It's The Law

Earlier in the book we talked about Florida's hurricane season. Buying a home in Florida during this time can present a problem almost all northerners are unaware of. Let's say you have closed on the sale of your home up north. You are now in Florida with everything you own in the moving truck. You are ready to close on your new home, move in and start living your Florida dream. You get a call, and are told you can't close because there are now active hurricanes (even though they are still far away) that forbid the insurance company from allowing the policy you have arranged to take effect. No insurance, no mortgage, no sale. It could be days, weeks, nobody knows. Now what do you do? You're literally homeless with all your personal belongings in an expensive moving truck and can't move in.

Why did this happen? In the past, there were people who would not insure their homes in order to save money. When a hurricane would approach their area, they would run out and get insurance real quick, only to cancel it once the threat had passed. This wasn't fair to the insurance company that could be on the hook for huge losses after collecting only one month's premium. It also wasn't fair to homeowners who paid for homeowners all along, and now have to endure higher rates to help cover the losses of all the people who just bought it at the last minute. So the State of Florida passed a law that prevents new insurance from being issued in any area when it becomes within a certain distance of a named storm.

During the busy hurricane seasons of 2004-2005, there were parts of the state that you could not get insurance for weeks at a time, because there was always one storm or another threatening. I often had buyers that were prevented from closing because of hurricanes. A retired couple that drove down here to close had to stay in a hotel for 12 days until insurance was allowed to take effect. It cost them thousands more than they counted on for accommodations, meals, and the additional days for storage and moving costs for their furniture.

Moves to Florida have also interrupted after a hurricane went through an area but before buyers were able to close on their home. When a hurricane causes damage in an area, the company that was going to cover you may now refuse to do so until they have a rep inspect the home to see if it has damage. The last thing an insurance company wants to do is insure a home that will have a large claim filed immediately. Getting someone from the company out to look at your home may take some time because the roads may be impassable and thousands of homes may have to be inspected. Situations like this can play havoc with the timing of the home you signed a contract to sell on a specific date.

Insurance Recap

When considering the purchase of a home in Florida, find out what it will cost to insure it before you sign an offer to purchase. The cost to insure your new property could be far higher than where you live now. Call an insurance agent directly, and you will become quickly educated on what insurances are required (if you are getting a mortgage) for that home. If it's in a high hazard flood zone (many areas in Florida are), you may need a copy of the elevation certificate for the home. On newer homes, the agent may be able to retrieve the elevation from a government website.

The rising cost of homeowners and flood insurance in Florida has forced people to leave the state in the past, so protect yourself and determine the total cost of ownership in Florida, including insurance, plus taxes, water and sewer and maintenance. Be aware that the total cost of living in Florida may rise faster than what you have been accustomed to in the past.

Here's a helpful tool provided by the Florida Office of Insurance Regulation. You can click on different counties in Florida to see the differences in insurance rates from area to area. Please note that the rates shown may not include all other required insurances such as flood, sinkhole, etc.

http://www.floir.com/choices/Home/Rates/4?id2=2

8. Different Demographics

Native Floridians

Living in Florida, you realize that most people you meet are not from the state originally. You can usually tell which folks were born and raised here in Florida. My guess is that showering and dentistry are recent to the state. Just kidding. Not all native Floridians look like their parents were cousins. Again, kidding. Many born Floridians provide general labor we need, like cutting the lawn or working in restaurants. Real Floridians are some of the nicest people you will ever meet, if you meet them before they've had their tenth beer of the day, which is hard to do unless you meet them early in the morning. Again, just.....OK let's move on.

Senior Citizens and Sightseeing Tourists

Have you ever sat behind a car that didn't move when

the light turned green? Ever had to wait because someone had their shopping cart in the middle of the aisle and didn't bother to move it when they saw you coming? How about being in a long line of cars in a no passing zone and the driver at front of the line is going way below the speed limit?

While living in Florida, you're like to be living in an area where there's a higher percentage of people who are in no particular hurry to get anywhere than where you live now. When living in such an area, you either adjust or go crazy. Chances are good that you will adjust to a slower pace of life. Taking it easy and relaxing is part of what the "Florida lifestyle" is about.

Moving to FL with Young Children

If most of what you know of Florida comes from visiting the theme parks or popular beaches, you may be in for a shock when you actually move here. The majority of your neighbors may be in their sixties, seventies, and eighties. This new scene may take some time to adjust to.

If you have young children and move into a neighborhood with a high percentage of seniors (which can be hard to avoid), your kids may not be too happy. Your children may not have many friends they can play and socialize with. Your next door neighbor in his eighties who has lived in the neighborhood years before you moved in, may get agitated when a baseball goes into his yard. Or when your son rides a bike on the street in front of his house, which your son has every right to do, but for some reason it upsets the neighbor.

Florida has a higher percentage of older residents than most other states, and that can affect the quality of your life, negatively or positively, depending upon what stage of life you're in. If you move your kids a thousand miles away from their old friends to an area where there aren't many kids at all, you may not be getting a "World's Greatest Dad" mug on Father's Day. If they become miserable, at least they will have one thing in common with that neighbor.

If You Are of Retirement Age

If you are retired, moving onto a street where the residents are of like age and mind may be exactly what will make you happy. Judging from the growth and popularity of 55 and older only communities, you would not be alone in wanting to avoid the problems that plagued Dennis the Menace's Mr. Wilson. There can be many other advantages than the absence of annoying little children (if that's how you feel) in those communities, such as maintenance free living where the lawn is cut and shrubs are taken care of by others. However, I have sold homes for seniors who moved out of 55+ communities because they hated living there, despite believing they would be perfect before moving in.

East is Fast, West is Slow

There are distinct differences between most of the east coast of Florida compared to the west coast. The differences are environmental as well as social. The water of the Atlantic Ocean on the east coast has bigger waves, frequent seaweed and can get deep quickly. On the west coast, the Gulf of Mexico water is usually clearer or translucent blue, warmer, and gentler. The I-95 corridor on the east has a faster pace, more northeast city-like. Along most of I-75 on the west, life has a slower tempo like the suburbs or country areas of northern states. East or west, the pace of life in Florida is slower overall than what you will find in a most comparably populated areas up north.

The Florida Lifestyle

When you live in Florida, you will hear a lot about the Florida lifestyle. Put a pool in and enjoy the Florida lifestyle. Elaborate outdoor furniture that duplicates your living room will allow you to enjoy the weather, nature and the Florida lifestyle. It's about rest, relaxation and reducing stress.

Life in Florida does have a slower pace, even in the cities and on the east coast. The beach towns and keys are where life is most relaxed. When you arrive at a restaurant near the beach at 11:30 am for lunch because that's when the sign says it'll open, but it doesn't for another twenty minutes, you learn what "keys time" is. The closer to the water you are, especially on the west coast' keys and islands, the more approximate posted times can be.

This slower way of life is just what many people are looking for. Others come here thinking that's what they want, but soon feel that eating dinner at four in the afternoon and seeing the streets deserted by nine is too slow.

Occasionally, the pace of life or demographic mix has been mentioned to me as one of the reasons for leaving. We all handle change differently. After moving to Florida, the differences in lifestyle that people expected was easier for people to adjust to, than the differences they didn't count on. For some, the number of unexpected things to adjust to after moving to Florida seemed to overwhelm them.

The more you know about the area in Florida you want to move to, the better. You can learn about the ages, education attained, etc. of the area you're moving to from the US Census website. If you've never explored the site, you may be amazed at how much you can quickly learn about any area. http://quickfacts.census.gov/qfd/states/12000.html

9. Save on Taxes

Real Estate Tax Homestead Savings

The Homestead Tax Protection Act provides unique tax benefits if the home you own in Florida is your principle or primary residence. The Homestead Act was designed to prevent homeowners from being taxed out of their home due to rising property values. Originally enacted to help seniors on a fixed retirement income, the law now benefits all Florida residents regardless of age. If you purchase a principle residence, you will not pay taxes on the first $50,000 of assessed value.

Every year, homestead exemptions are set by how the property is owned on the first day of January. In Florida, real estate taxes are paid in "arrears," so they are due at the end of the year. For instance, if you buy a home in June, it's already been decided if that property will benefit from the homestead exemption for the taxes due on it at the end of the year. If it was exempted on January first of that year, you would not be taxed on the first $50,000 of value. If the property does not have the exemption, you will pay the full tax for that year. To get the exemption for the following year, you must own the home by January first and apply for the exemption by March 1st.

From MyFlorida.com, the State of Florida official website, "Every person who owns and resides on real property in Florida on January 1 and makes the property his or her permanent residence is eligible to receive a homestead exemption up to $50,000. The first $25,000 applies to all property taxes, including school district taxes. The additional exemption up to $25,000, applies to the assessed value between $50,000 and $75,000 and only to non-school taxes." Additional exemptions may be available for widowers and people with disabilities or military service.

You can't get the homestead exemption on any non-owner occupied properties. If you buy a two unit home and rent both units out, there is no exemption. If you live in one unit and rent the other one out, you can get the entire property exempted if it's your principle residence.

You can apply for the exemption at the property appraisers office of the county in which your home is located. You will need the following documentation to apply for the exemption:

1. A copy of the warranty deed you received at closing when you bought the property to prove you own it.

2. Florida driver's licenses for all owners with the address of the property to be homesteaded matching the address on the license. If you don't drive you'll need a "Declaration of Domicile" (which you can get from the county or print it from their website if available) or a voter's registration card instead of a driver's license.

3. Florida registrations for any vehicles owned, matching the property address.

4. Social Security numbers of all owners.

As soon as you move to Florida, whether you buy or rent, the state wants you to get a Florida driver's license and Florida registration for all vehicles. The cost to get your car registration may be more than where you moved from. The cost shocked me when I first moved there. Florida auto insurance was higher too. All those partying tourists in rental cars they're unfamiliar with, driving in unfamiliar areas?

Additional Exemptions if You Qualify

An additional $50,000 exemption may be available for you if you are 65 or older. In order to qualify, you must:

1. Have been approved for the first $50,000 exemption.

2. Have an adjusted gross household income lower than the amount that Florida sets each year. It was just under $30,000 for 2012.

You can get the exact income amount from the county when you apply for the regular exemption. You must apply in person usually and provide proof of age, of course, and show tax return and any wage or other income source documents.

There are additional exemptions for a widow or widower, members of the military and the disabled if you qualify. You can get details and updates on changes from the State of Florida here: http://dor.myflorida.com/dor/property/taxpayers/ex emptions.html

No Individual State Income Tax in Florida

Most states in the U.S. require you to pay a tax on your income to them, in addition to what you pay to the IRS for federal tax. Most states take between three and ten percent. Some states offer a break to seniors or the disabled. Florida does not charge any citizen a tax on their individual income. Keeping more of your income is nice, and not even having to prepare a state return every year is better.

Thinking of maintaining two or more homes in different states? Consult a qualified professional because, financially, it may be best to make your home in Florida your principle residence and use the other place as a vacation home. You could save lots of money on income taxes and get better protection of your assets (covered later).

A Benefit When Home Values Drop

Another good thing about Florida is the way they reassess the value of properties on a yearly basis. Every year the property appraisers adjust the value of all properties in the county according to a formula that measures if property has gone up or down in value. Many states will increase your assessment and tax as values rise, but neglect to lower your taxes when values go down. Florida has a more taxpayer friendly system.

During Florida's frequent housing busts, I was relieved to see the real estate taxes on my home go down substantially when the value did. The same did not happen when I owned homes up north. In fact, in areas where the prices dropped dramatically in that northern state, the still high property taxes were often the reason properties would not sell. Buyers would see a bargain price on a property, but couldn't afford to buy it because of the high real estate taxes based on an outdated high assessment.

10. Best Asset Protection State

What is Asset Protection

Asset protection can refer to a number of different subjects, but this chapter is about passive asset protection. All you have to do is move to Florida, become a resident, and you will automatically enjoy all of the protections discussed in this chapter. Florida is in the top three states in the US for laws that protect its citizens' assets.

Unlimited Protection Your Home Equity

When you become a Florida resident homeowner, the equity in your home is protected from creditors regardless of how valuable your home is. For example, you move to Florida and buy a home for $250,000. You get a Florida driver's license and register your car in the state and register to vote. You now consider yourself a resident of Florida and your home your principle residence. It is now almost impossible for any potential creditors to touch your equity in that home or attach a judgment to it.

After becoming a resident, let's say you happen upon some bad financial luck such as a credit card balance you can't pay, or you are involved in an automobile accident and get sued. Even if they get a judgment against you, they can't come after your home to pay for it. In Florida, your qualifying principle residence is exempt, off limits. In many other states, the judgment would attach to your home, and they could force the sale of your home to pay the debt.

This is an unlimited exemption that covers your qualifying principle residence. All of your equity is protected whether it is $5,000 or $500,000. Most other states provide little or no such protection.

Not All Properties Qualify

You may never need it, but this protection will give you free added financial security, so you may want to make sure that the property you purchase will qualify. For a home to qualify in an incorporated municipality (city or town), the property must not be on more than a half acre.

In rural areas outside the city limits, the exemption allows up to 160 acres. How can you tell if an area is an incorporated municipality? If it has its own governmental agencies like its own police force, mayor and other city services, it probably is. We are talking about cities and towns, not counties.

I lived in a town that had its own name and zip code, but it was not an incorporated municipality. All services were provided by the county. The county's sheriff and deputies provided law enforcement. The 160 acre rule applied there.

If you will have substantial equity in your Florida home or operate a business that has a higher chance of being sued by trial lawyers, be sure to verify that any property you buy will qualify before you sign anything.

100% Protection of Your IRA and Other Qualified Retirement Funds

If you've worked and made sacrifices necessary to put money away in your 401(k), IRA or other retirement savings plan, the last thing you want is an overzealous litigation attorney to file a law suit because of an accident or other misfortune and take everything you have in your retirement accounts.

In most states, creditors can go after your retirement funds because there is little or no protection provided by law. Some states open the entire amount to creditors. Others protect only the amount that is needed for reasonable support. What is "reasonably needed for support"? That is open to the discretion of the judge in the case. The possibility that your life savings could be taken from you may be a powerful reason to look at moving to a state that provides more respect of your retirement assets, like Florida.

If you become a Florida resident, just like the homestead exemption for your home, your retirement funds will be exempt from attachment by creditors. This exemption is also unlimited, which means your funds are protected whether the amount is a thousand or million. Talk about financial security, peace of mind and being able to sleep at night.

As with the Florida homestead protection, there are guidelines that can affect this otherwise wonderful protection. Your retirement funds may have to be held by a "Florida only" financial institution, because only funds held in the state may be exempt. If you live in New York and move your assets to Florida after you have been sued, they may not be protected. If you are moving to Florida and you want to know what your protection rights are under the law, contact a Florida attorney for advice before you move. I have provided some contact information in the resource section in the back of the book.

Life Insurance Cash Value and Proceeds Protected

Do you have a life insurance policy? Is there some cash value to the policy, such as with a whole life or a universal policy? If so, the entire value of the policy could be out of the reach of creditors once you are a Florida resident. The proceeds of the life insurance policy are also exempt from creditors of the policy owner. This is another protection to keep in mind because many other states offer no such thing.

Annuities Protected Too

According to Investorpedia.com, the definition of an

annuity is a financial product that can provide a steady income to its owners, usually for the entire life of the owner. There are many different types, but financial institutions, such as insurance companies, offer these to people who are interested in securing additional steady income from money they have to invest. They are popular with those who are approaching or already enjoying retirement.

Many other states allow creditors to take all of this income to satisfy claims. Here again, Florida residents are afforded rare protection of 100% of this income from creditors.

Protection in Bankruptcy for Floridians

Florida's excellent financial protection of its citizens even extends to bankruptcy. The amount of property you can keep after filing for bankruptcy is different from state to state. The state of Florida has opted out of the regular federal property and asset exemptions and allows its citizens to keep more than any other state, according to Florida attorneys.

One of the largest exemptions is your home. The Florida constitution allows you to keep all of the equity in your home, even if it is worth a million dollars. Any state that forces their citizens to use the regular federal bankruptcy exemptions may only be able to keep up to $22,000. Obviously, if you are moving to the state and are going to be purchasing a home with cash, knowing this equity is protected from financial calamities can be extremely comforting.

Bankruptcy laws went through a major revision in 2005. In order to use the unlimited protection for your home, you have to be a Florida Resident for 3.3 years first. However, your equity may be fully protected for those 3.3 years by the regular homestead equity protection that we talked about, until you do file. Consult a Florida attorney for specifics.

Decision Help: If you are overly concerned about the safety of your money, the state of Florida offers its residents the best automatic protection of your assets of all US states (Texas asset protection laws are similar) right out of the box without the need for trusts and complicated financial mechanisms. If it's a tossup between which state to live in and you have substantial net worth, or your retirement would be shattered by a huge award in at the hands of a trial lawyer, becoming a Florida resident may give you much better protection and peace of mind.

Disclaimer Reminder

The information in this book is provided to make you aware of the possible additional benefits of becoming a Florida resident, but it is not professional or legal advice. To find out more about asset protection and how it may benefit you personally, contact a qualified Florida Attorney or CPA whose practice includes this field. A list of Florida licensed professionals can be found in the "resources" section in the back of this book merely as general information and are not recommendations or endorsements.

11. Florida Living Options

Sell Everything and Move to Florida Full Time

Selling everything and moving to "paradise" has a lot of appeal. A move to full-time Florida living warrants the most thought because it will expose you to everything about Florida you moved there for, and all the negatives, many of which are hard to imagine until you live there. The data shows that your chances of satisfaction with your full time relocation long term are not good.

This is What You Want to Avoid

$15,000 Money lost on real estate commission, closing cost on home sale to move to FL.

$5,000 Money lost to move belongings to FL.

$5,000 Money lost in closing cost, inspections, etc. on

FL home purchase.

$15,000 Money lost on real estate commission, closing cost on FL home sale to move to out.

$5,000 Money lost in closing cost, inspections, etc. on home purchase in new location.

$5,000 Money lost to move belongings to new location.

$50,000 Total Money lost *Note: Round numbers that are easy to add were used and are intended as an example only.*

Florida residential real estate values rise and fall farther and faster. It's quite possible the home you purchase in Florida today will be worth $50,000 more or less at the time you want to sell. If in the case above if it was lower, your total loss would be $100,000. I have seen real people lose much more than that. In a ten year period, I saw one builder's model sell for somewhere between $69,900 and $239,900. I mean the same exact home with the lot and everything. The value did not just go up. It would go up, down, up, then down again.

Some buyers who paid over $200,000 for this home when the market was OK would have a hard time getting $100,00 three years later in one period. The prices dropped that much, that fast. The builder didn't stop building during slow markets. He just lowered his price, sometimes dropping the price $10,000 a month. What most people don't know, even many realtors, is that when home prices drop, the cost of lots can drop even faster. A builder who has been paying $50,000 for lots in some areas during a good market can often buy similar lots for only $5,000 two years later during a Florida bust. So he can drop the price of his new home $45,000 and still make the same profit. You, as a home owner, don't enjoy that same advantage. How are you going to get $200,000 (what you paid) when the builder is advertising the same home, brand new for $155,000? So is it possible to move to Florida, realize you made a mistake and lose a lot of money when you have to sell? Absolutely.

The only reason home prices go up is that there is more demand than there is supply to go around. Prices go down when there are more sellers than buyers. In 2008, everyone wanted to sell in Florida, but no one wanted to buy, so real estate values dropped about 60%. My point is that most people sell when prices are low, and they are low because so many want to sell at the same time. So chances are your move will not work out, and you will want to sell when prices are lower. This is what commonly happens, but this is what we want to avoid.

Losing money is one thing, but many sellers told me the emotional cost was even worse, especially for older folks and families with children still in school. Two long distance moves and multiple real estate transactions is not only very stressful, it's a huge disruption to the enjoyment of life. Is that what you want to be spending years of your retirement doing? If you have a young family, moving children in and out of schools and neighborhoods can have negative long term consequences.

The Right Time to Buy in Florida

What happens if you move to Florida and it happens to be the *right* time? It has been my experience that when people move to Florida at the *right* time and buy a home, if the Florida dream doesn't work out but they can sell for a nice PROFIT and leave, the whole ordeal is much easier to take.

If you move to Florida and buy when the real estate market is down, you are buying at the right time because by the time things that chase people out of Florida happen to you, chances are you will be able to sell that home for a profit. Making a profit (even if by dumb luck) when you make a mistake can take some of the sting out of it. The problem is that it's almost never the right time.

I have been negative on Florida real estate since 2005. At that time, after two straight hurricane seasons, I saw the number of new listings start to exceed the new sales by a wide margin every month. Real estate prices are all about supply and demand. As I watched the inventory picture change abruptly, I noticed that almost no one else did. I was helping investors buy, remodel and resell at a profit and checked the inventory almost hourly. I saw the market turn negative and yet a well known economist was proclaiming that most homes in Florida were going to sell above the $1,000,000 mark in five years. It was shortly after that proclamation that the Florida housing market experienced its worse decline since the depression. The only difference between most fortune tellers and economists is the latter have a degree.

The point is that I watched as inventory grew and prices dropped by half. I've been negative on Florida real estate strictly from the view of it as a product from October 2005. People who bought a home in Florida in the few years before 2005 paid too much. It's been the *wrong* time to buy for a decade.

Now, it's becoming more obvious daily that the bottom of the historic drop in prices in Florida that happened during the great recession has been hit. Historically, that means Florida is at the beginning stage of boom in real estate prices. While this next price rise may be milder, 2013 may be the *right* time to buy, because I believe prices will be considerably higher in three to five years. Most of the last ten years was not a good time and in just a couple of years it will be riskier.

No one should move to Florida or anywhere without careful research. However, if you've considered everything and are going to go, moving to Florida before prices rise too much could at least prevent you from experiencing a big financial loss if your relocation doesn't work out. If you buy this year, chances are better that when you sell in the future, it will be for a profit.

About Moving Mainly to Escape Cold Weather

If you hate cold weather and snow, and think about

moving to Florida mainly during the winter months, there may be better options than moving to Florida. Remember, Florida isn't warm and sunny all the time. Most of the year it's hot and humid. If you hate winter but you also can't stand stretches of humid weather in the summer, trading three months of winter (where you are now) for six to nine months of sticky, humid Florida weather may turn out to be one decision you'll regret.

What to do? The weather in Florida during the winter is truly spectacular. It's usually warm, not hot. Oppressive humidity is gone. It rarely rains. They don't make hurricanes this time of year either. Yes, from sometime in November to sometime in March, Florida is paradise in most of the state. You don't need to run the AC. You can leave doors and windows open and enjoy fresh air throughout your home. You can dine outside without sweating into your BBQ.

So yes, I completely understand if you're reading this book and it's cold outside, and you have to go out into a gray day and shovel snow surrounded by trees without leaves and wishing that you were laying in a hammock in the Florida sun instead. For you, there may be better options than moving to Florida to live full-time.

Cold Weather Escape Option One

Some of the happiest people I've met over the years are what Floridians call snowbirds. Snowbirds are northerners who migrate to Florida every year to escape the cold weather up north, and then return home when the weather is nice. Snowbirds can rent or own, but we're going to discuss renting first.

Seasonal rentals are fully furnished homes or condos that are *not* rented out on an annual basis. Most are offered for rent on a monthly basis with only a one month minimum rental. These are often advertised as "turnkeys," meaning you just bring your clothes and toothbrush and you have a new home for a month or more. Usually all maintenance, utilities and lawn care are included in the price. You can easily find seasonal rentals just about anywhere in Florida.

If the main reason you have thoughts of moving to Florida is to avoid a cold winter, and certainly if that is the only reason, becoming a snowbird may be your best bet. I have met many people who only live in Florida for one month every year. January seems to be the preferred month. One couple explained it this way: they can spend the holidays like Thanksgiving at the end of November and Christmas a month later with the family and maybe even enjoy seeing the first snow. Then on January 1st they head to Florida for a month. The weather in November and December in northern U.S. areas is rarely very brutal anymore. Spending the holidays with old friends and your family is important to most people.

For many, a break from the cold for just the month of January seems to be all the escape they need. When they return north, February isn't that hard to take because they just spent a month in paradise. Just when the cold starts to become bothersome, spring weather and the return of leaves and flowers kicks in.

If you find that staying in Florida for just the month of January doesn't offer the retreat from the cold you need, you could always stay January and February and see if that does it for you. Many snowbirds make arrangements to stay at the same place year after year if they liked the home and the location.

There are many advantages of living in Florida for just a month or more in a seasonal rental while keeping the home you are in now. It's really not that expensive. If you're a smart shopper, you can stay for a month in Florida seasonal home for the same cost many people spend on just a week's vacation. If you find that you want to spend January through March in Florida, then you should consider the pros and cons of buying verses renting. Renting first is probably the smartest move even if you eventually move to Florida full-time. You will learn what really works best for you: number of months, condo or home, on the beach or a half hour away, etc.

If you do go the seasonal rental route and find that you like staying in Florida three months or more each year, it may make more sense to purchase a winter home, rather than rent. If you are going to be spending that much time in Florida, you may want to downsize your northern home.

The weather in Florida during the calendar winter months is fantastic, normally. Warm, not hot and humid, with little or no rain and sunshine all day long is normal for most of the state. Weather patterns have been more unpredictable lately, and some recent Florida winters have seen an increase in cloudy rainy days.

I do suggest you rent first and start with the smallest home or condo you think would be comfortable with. You will be spending a lot of time outdoors. Look for a place with a nice size private outdoor space (screened lanai) for you to soak up the sun or enjoy a meal in the fresh air. Renting a condo on the third floor without a balcony means you will always have to go to a public area to enjoy the outdoors.

Owning in Florida and Your Home State

In talking with thousands of people who have moved to Florida, the folks with a home in Florida and their home state are by far the happiest with their living arrangements. They feel more connected to the state where they have lots of family, friends and roots. Many still own the same home they have lived in a long time up north, and some have sold that home and downsized.

We'll call them "sixers" for the rest of this book because most of them spend about six months a year at each home. Most are retired couples with the freedom to travel when and where they wish. I have also met self employed individuals who have figured out how to achieve freedom of movement while continuing to earn income, thanks mainly to the internet.

Many sixers start arriving in Florida in October or November, but some spend the holidays up north and head south after Christmas. They come down here and enjoy the best weather Florida has to offer. It is warm and sunny with little or no rain or humidity. The snakes and gators are less active. Bugs are less of a factor, probably because many additional birds come here to escape the cold northern winter and they snack on them. Best of all, there are no hurricanes and no evacuations.

After sixers have had their fun at the golf courses, theme parks, and beaches, they go back north just in time for spring. Some follow a strict pattern, and many let the weather tell them when to go back and forth. I know a retired couple that has a cabin style home in the mountains of northern Michigan and a nice home here. When it starts to get too cold for their taste up north, they come to Florida. When the humidity starts to bother them as they play tennis, they head north.

I know other Floridians that leave when hurricane season starts. They stay north through the summer and spend Thanksgiving and Christmas with the family. They head to Florida after New Year's Day. If you ever traveled I-95 heading south in the beginning of January, you no doubt noticed many more cars, boats and RV's heading south.

The reason the sixers are so happy is obvious to full time Floridians. The sixers enjoy the best Florida has to offer. They come down when the weather is warm and the nights are cool, good sleeping weather. You rarely will have to use the heat or AC. There's no daily stress from watching a huge hurricane slowly making its menacing advances toward you. The lines at the theme parks (except holidays) are shorter and it's cooler. You can enjoy being outside all day without drowning in your own sweat. For sixers, Florida is just like the travel brochures.

While enjoying the best time of year in Florida, they also escaped winter back home. They did not have to shovel snow. They did not suffer the depressing cold sunless days looking out at leafless trees. Then, as the weather in Florida starts to turn hot, humid and hurricane season approaches, the sixers head north. Arriving north, they are greeted by the blooming spring flowers and leaves shooting out of tree branches. The days are warm and nights cool. Ah, the good life.

Sixers don't suffer depression from feeling separated or isolated from old family and friends. They easily arrange to spend the holidays that are most important to them with the family. What the sixers have figured out is how to enjoy the best of back home and Florida, and avoiding the drawbacks of each.

The first thing most of these happy contented sixers did was buy a home in Florida. They became Florida residents by getting a driver's license, registering their cars and using their new Florida address as their principle residence when filling out their Federal tax returns. They now enjoy all the asset protection benefits discussed earlier and are free from paying state income tax.

How to Afford Two Homes the Same as One

Some sixers still have the home up north they've had for years. Others sold that big home and used the cash to buy two less expensive homes, a smaller one near their family and a Florida home. It may be more affordable than you think. Replace your $300,000 home with a $150,000 home up north and in Florida. Make Florida your principle residence to reap the tax and asset protection benefits. Spend winter in FL where you won't need to pay to heat or cool the home, while saving up north by keeping the thermostat just warm enough so the pipes don't freeze. Many people have told me they now maintain two homes for what it cost for just one before.

The Florida Home and Motorhome Option

Another option that works well for some people having a motorhome instead of a home up north. When the weather in Florida starts to turn muggy and hurricane season beckons, they travel to more desirable destinations. Many do this for three or more months every year. Some find a resort they love and stay there year after year. Others travel throughout the U.S. and Canada, seeking out the most interesting places. I'm told it sure beats staying inside and watching eight hours of mind numbing low quality TV every day. Most RV owners have told me they've met lots of wonderful new friends and meet up and travel with some of the same ones every year.

Traveling back home from for visits and evacuating in

a motorhome is more comfortable than travel by car. You always have a comfortable place to stay that's free of bedbugs and stocked with food and drink. You can pull over to eat or sleep just about any time you wish. I'm told to be sure to get one with its own generator, so you can be completely self sufficient because it can power everything from the fridge to the AC when you pull off the road and shut the engine off.

Keeping your home up north and buying a motorhome to stay in Florida during the winter is another popular option, although this choice does not provide the benefits afforded Florida residents. Many people find a RV resort in Florida they love and stay at that same resort every winter for years. Some of the best located resorts are booked solid for years, so researching availability is recommended before buying an RV if you are only interested in staying in a particular area in Florida.

What would make you happiest? Having a complete change of scenery to look forward to every year keeps life interesting. Goldilocks might have been on to something because some of the happiest people I met in Florida never stay where it's too cold or too hot and humid.

A Test for Potential Full Time Florida Residents

Just about anywhere in Florida you can find seasonal rental homes to rent by the month. If your plans are full-time Florida living, consider finding a seasonal rental in the area that you would like to move to and test renting there first if you can. While these fully furnished homes may command top dollar during the winter, they can usually be rented at a huge discount the rest of the year because they often just sit vacant. Rent a home or condo similar to what you want to buy. During a test, you want to learn what it really would be like to live in a state with six to nine months of summer.

Rent for at least six months if you can, anywhere from April 15th through October 15th at a minimum. A test period of a year would be good, but a period from around April 1st through January 1st where you don't travel home for the holidays or have visitors from back home would be ideal. If you live in Florida long enough, there will be a time when you won't be able to spend holidays with family or friends up north. However, if a shorter test is what you must do, just make sure it DOES NOT include the winter months from December through March.

If you are saying, hold on now, isn't this going to cost a lot of money? Yes, but this test will cost you pennies on the dollar compared to moving to Florida, hating it and moving back, if you are going to sell and buy a home to do it. If you rent, a test isn't needed, just go for it if that's what you think is best.

For owners, beginning a test on April 15th will hopefully test another major reason for dissatisfaction: missing your family and the get-togethers. You will be in Florida for Memorial Day,

Fourth of July and Labor Day. If your family normally gets together for picnics or other celebrations for these holidays, you will be forced to miss them, or go through the expense and hassle or frequent trips back home. Try putting up with airport security or the traffic on I-95 for multiple round trips in a three month period. Keep in mind that later in the year you have Thanksgiving, Christmas and New years in a two month period.

You may be thinking, well maybe the family will come down to Florida to visit us for the Fourth of July. We can all go to the beach, or Disney, and it will be great. Try to resist. This is supposed to be a test of what living in Florida long term will really be like. Ask anyone who has lived in Florida for years, and they will tell you that the family will want to come down. They will come down on vacation and you will have a wonderful time, in the beginning. After the first couple of years, the visits become less frequent. The travel time, hassle and expense and repeating the same vacation over and over will become less appealing. Besides, you'll be living in Florida full-time and regret it so you'll become crabby and not someone they will look forward to seeing (just kidding, of course, this doesn't happen to everyone).

For the purposes of this test, don't let the family visit. If you want to see them, you do the traveling because that is what it is going to be like the longer you live in Florida and everyone else stays up north. You need to test this to see what it is really like because this is another major reason why all those people who made a permanent move to Florida moved back.

Sixers Test

Planning on buying in Florida, but also maintaining a home up north too? Congratulations! Chances are that not only will you be happy with that decision, but it may also help you stay healthier and enjoy a longer life. I have not found any studies on this, but this was the lifestyle of most of the healthiest older people I met in Florida.

Since this choice will probably work long term, the focus of your test should be to determine what area and type of property would be best. If the thought of condo living interests you, but you never lived in one longer than a week on vacation, now would be the time to test that out.

While choosing a condo for full-time Florida living turned out to be a disaster for buyers who had always lived in single family homes previously, it was less of an issue when they were only going to use it six months or less a year. Many still didn't like all the condo rules or fees, but being able to lock the door and head north anytime they wanted without having to worry about any maintenance made up for it. In some areas of Florida, a condo can be a less expensive option to living in a more desirable location, like on the beach.

If you're not sure what area in Florida to choose, use the internet to research. A blog I have at http://StateofFloridaLiving.com may help. Avoid asking a real estate agent who only sells in one particular area, because that's always the best area no matter which town it is. I would also stay away from forums, as they are mostly populated with agents, some even posing as non-agents who are quick to recommend the area and agent (themselves or a relative). Through research, try to narrow it down to three areas or less. Plan a trip spending a full month in each of the areas. Try to stay in seasonal rentals, fully furnished homes and condos located in regular residential areas similar to where you would buy. You'll learn about grocery stores, traffic, golf courses etc., and get a snapshot of what living there would be like. Spending a full month in a home or condo with regular Florida residents as neighbors will give you a better feel for the place than if you stayed in a hotel and lived like tourist.

How Not to Test Full-Time Florida Living

Do not test full-time Florida living in December through March, because it will just convince you to move. You might as well just move and save the money you would have spent on a trial run during the winter months. If you make a decision to live in Florida as a full time resident based on being here during only the winter, you could be setting yourself up for a huge mistake. That would be like someone making a decision to move where you live now based upon a stay there during May. They wouldn't be getting the full picture.

Not one seller ever told me they wanted out from

Florida because of the winter here. Sure, there are complaints from full-time Floridians due to the influx of snowbirds. The traffic is worse with all the additional cars with out of state plates going half the speed limit, stopping in the middle of the street without warning to gawk at something, and of course driving straight for miles with a turn signal on (not really, that's common year round). The golf courses are far more crowded, as are the beaches, restaurants and stores. Standing in a line just to get into any restaurant that has average or better food in many areas is common. These are just minor inconveniences really, that are easily tolerated because of the glorious weather, and they don't seem to bother the snowbirds or the sixers. Florida in the winter is likely everything you've dreamed about.

A test is where you would live in the area you are considering through at least the worst six months of Florida summer weather. Experience the excitement of hurricane season. Maybe you'll be lucky enough to be ordered to evacuate. The goal is to experience some of the worst parts of full time Florida living. Tropical storms, wild fires, swarms of bugs, heat, humidity, alligators, snakes and watching a hurricane as big as the state itself approach. Can it really be all that bad? That's the purpose of the trial, to find out before you make a commitment that could cost a fortune in time and money to reverse.

12. Useful Tips on Buying

Condo or Single Family Home

You probably have a snapshot in your mind of what you want your new Florida life to look like. Let me tell you how some common dreams of how Florida life turned out for some when it became reality. We can learn by making mistakes, but it's better to learn from the mistakes of others if possible.

The first dream we are going to dissect is the "condo" dream. In this picture, you sell your up north home and snow shovel and move to a condo in Florida and retire. While living in this condo, everything will be taken care of for you. You won't have to cut the grass, trim bushes, paint or fix anything outside anymore. Now that you are retired, you can just lie leisurely in a hammock and watch someone else do the work. You won't have a care in the world. Well, not exactly.

While it may be true that you may not have to do any of the outside maintenance or repairs, you will be paying for it in the monthly condo fee. This is over and above your mortgage payment (if any), taxes, and insurance. You could live in a single family home and pay to have someone else take care of those very same things for the same cost, but probably much less. The difference is you will have control over the cost and how things are done in your own single family home, but little or no control in a condo.

In a home, you could have the lawn cut for you but choose to take care of the flowerbeds and minor trimming yourself. Many people find working around the yard or tending to a garden or flower bed at a leisurely pace very relaxing. It gets you outside for a little exercise. Many get satisfaction from having a manicured property that they had a hand in bringing about. You can't do that in a condo. I've had people who moved from a condo after only a few months tell me neighbors filed a complaint against them for putting a potted flower right outside "their" front door to brighten things up. They quickly found that "theirs" ends at the door.

In your condo dream, you are lying in a hammock with a cool drink and maybe taking in an afternoon nap in the fresh air. That may not happen as you plan. First of all, you probably won't be allowed to put a hammock up, as it could be against the condo rules. If the condo association provides them, which is rare anymore (liability issues), there may only be two of them for the use of 600 residents. If you ever get to use them, your time may be limited, and they may be located in a noisy, overcrowded rec area. Reading that novel or taking a nap may not be possible.

Avoiding a Condo Dream Turned Nightmare

If you have lived in your own single family home for the last couple of decades, moving to a condo may not be something you will ever adjust to. I have sold many condos for owners who only lived there a short time because actually living in a condo wasn't at all how they pictured it. For most, they didn't realize they only control what happens inside their walls and have to strictly follow the book of rules on what happens the minute they step outside. Some sellers told me that almost every day since they moved in, they were told about something else they weren't allowed to do. They didn't care how much money they might lose, they wanted to sell and sell now. They quickly realized they needed a home where they can do what they want, just like they have done for most of their lives.

In another case, I helped a widow get a great deal on a large condo on the beach. She wanted a condo so all the outdoor chores would be done for her. I found out later that she was looking forward to plenty of visits from her family, and that's why she wanted a large condo, even though it was just her.

The very first time one of those family visits took place, the weaknesses in her plan showed. The grandkids felt cooped up inside the condo and wanted to go outside and play. So they went to the condo's pool. They went back and forth to the beach. They left their sandy flip-flops and sneakers outside the front door so they wouldn't track sand inside. The widow saw nothing wrong in any of this. Her neighbors, however, did. Numerous complaints were filed against her with the condo association. Too much noise. Can't leave personal items outside your front door. All children on the property must be accompanied by an adult at all times. That ruined what was supposed to the first of many memorable family visits for her. She called me to put the condo up for sale the day after her family went back home. She sold and moved back.

Can You Back Out of a Sale?

If you make an offer on a condo in the state of Florida, you have a three day right of rescission that begins after you get the condo docs. This gives you time to learn all of the rules, regulations and restrictions imposed on your use of the property. You have the right to back out of the contract if you don't like what you find, if you do so within the three days allowed. The problem is that the documents can be a hundred pages and very confusing. Most buyers don't find it very good reading. Often, they never read much of it and don't understand exactly what they are signing up for.

If you are buying a condo for the first time, make sure you read everything. Write down all of your questions. Make notes of everything you don't understand. You deserve to get correct answers to all of your questions and learn if there are restrictions that you will not be able to live with. I would get answers from the people at the condo association office, not the sellers. I would not ask the realtor unless they were a resident of the condo complex and you trust them. I would also do this by email, so I would have the answers in writing.

If you enjoy the freedom of doing what you like, when you like, with the property you own, you probably won't like condo living. If you have lived in a condo or apartment in a large city for most of your life, then it probably won't be an issue for you. If you are buying a condo to live in six months or less a year, that may work well for you, even if you never lived in one before. But why guess? Rent one for a month in the complex before committing to a purchase if you can.

Deed Restrictions

The State of Florida is filled with subdivisions and communities where the home you purchase may be subject to deed restrictions. Deed restrictions are limits and rules on what you can do with and to your property, in addition to the normal government permitting, zoning and code restrictions you may be familiar with. You can usually tell when you are entering a deed restricted area because most have a gate or other special entrance you must pass through to get in, although some don't. They usually have a Homeowners Association (HOA) similar to a condo association that enforces the rules.

Deed restrictions will limit what you can do with your single family home on its own lot, so it would be wise to find out what those limitations are before you sign an offer. Like purchasing a condo, there is a disclosure that must be provided to a buyer who is buying a home in a HOA area that discloses that fact. The disclosure tells you what the associated fees are and that there *may* be restrictions on its use. It also allows a buyer to cancel the deal if the disclosure is not given.

Unlike a condo disclosure, however, the HOA disclosure has no requirement (at this time) that the buyer receive the HOA documents so you can learn what the deed restrictions are or how the association is run. HOA disclosure law is more recent than Condo disclosure laws and doesn't provide the same protection yet, although I see that changing in the future. Make sure you get a copy of the deed restrictions before you sign an offer.

I would not rely on an answer from a real estate agent unless I have very good reason to trust them (they're your brother, for instance). A realtor may not have any facts on the restrictions at all or base it on hearsay. Almost all agreements of sale you'll be asked to sign to buy a property state that the written papers you sign are what matter, and you aren't relying on oral representations. So being told something that turns out not to be true probably won't stand up in court.

Don't make the same mistake as many others and become the proud owner of a home that you can't do something you intended to. A good agent will help you get the facts on paper to read before you sign an agreement of sale. If you sign an agreement with the basic disclosure included and find out later you don't like the restrictions, there may be little you can do about it.

There are many communities that have been built to have a Mediterranean look and feel about them. A deed restriction in one of these areas could be that all homes must have a tile roof. Maybe the tile roof must also be a certain color so all the homes are uniform and fit the desired look of the community. Let's say you buy in this area and later need a new roof. You get estimates. You're told that you can have a nice new shingle roof put on for $15,000, but the red tile roof required by this community will set you back $40,000. This one restriction alone is going to cost you $25,000, but you won't have a choice. You gave up that right when you bought the home.

Deed restrictions are enacted to protect property values of the homes in the community. They can be a very good thing if none of the restrictions interfere with your intended use of the home. One home I owned was in a non-gated deed restricted area that did not restrict roof choices. It had restrictions that I thought were great and some that I found ridiculous. One restriction that irked some of my neighbors was that your garage door couldn't be open longer than an hour. The drafters decided a community looked neater with all the garage doors closed, so you don't have to look at other people's garage junk.

A drive through some non-restricted communities show the advantages of living in a deed restricted area if you prefer to live in an area that's nice and neat. Many non-restricted areas have large, beautiful homes with manicured lawns, and right next door are small, maintenance neglected homes with rusted cars and other junk in the front yard. If you invest in a good size home and later someone builds a very small home right next to you, that can negatively affect your property value. Bottom line, when looking at homes in an area, always be aware what the restrictions are, if any, and if they are right for you.

Caged Pool Home, Yes or No?

This is a difficult question to give advice on because it really is just personal choice, but I can tell you how other buyers' choices have worked out. First, above ground pools are not looked upon very highly in most of Florida. So when we talk about pools, we are talking about in-ground pools. Above ground pools generally will not even be allowed in many areas. Where they are allowed, they can be a liability. Tropical storms and hurricanes can flatten them or rip them apart and turn their parts into projectiles. They can cause a home to sell slower and for a lower price because most sellers want a caged in-ground pool, and removing an above ground pool is a hassle that leaves a large grass-less area.

If you are considering the southern two thirds of the state, we will also assume that we are talking about "caged" in ground pools. A caged pool has a cool deck (patio-like floor that doesn't get hot like concrete can) poured around it, with a large frame surrounding the entire pool area allowing it to be screened in. This screened cage keeps all the bad stuff like mosquitoes and leaves out of your pool area. It makes the entire pool area seem more like an extension of your interior of your home because of this physical barrier between the pool area and the outside world.

The pool cage, in combination with the lanai (roofed patio screened in with the same materials as the pool cage), provide you with a large bug free area to enjoy the outdoors. This space feels like interior living space, but it's outdoors. During the winter you may spend more time outside in this space than inside. Some people have outdoor living room furniture, stereo systems and flat screen TVs set up out there. This is one reason you may not need such a large home in FL, since you may be spending more time in this outdoor area. This does not apply to the six or more months of a humid weather if you stay here year round.

This cage also allows you to keep the sliding glass doors to your home wide open when the weather is beautiful. Many Florida homes have multiple pocketing sliding glass doors. When you fully open these, it's like removing a wall and opening your entire home to the outside.

Pools are taken much more seriously in Florida because you can often swim all year. You never close the pool. In areas where almost all of the pools are caged, avoid pools without a cage to protect your resale value. The first time most buyers walk through a Florida style home and pass through the sliding glass doors onto the screened lanai and caged pool area, they're hooked. Since this area is so large for the relatively low additional cost per square foot of area it adds to a home, similar size homes without a caged pool just don't seem to compare.

Now, Should You Buy a Home With a Pool?

When I show homes to buyers in the six to nine months when it's hot and humid, almost everyone wants a pool home. When showing homes in the winter when it's seventy degrees with lower humidity, it isn't as important to them at that moment. In my opinion, buyers allow themselves to be influenced too much by the weather at that time when making a decision. Too often, Florida home buyers are under pressure to buy now, because their home back north is under contract and they need a place to move into in four weeks.

Many who buy a home without a pool because it was cool when they were shopping for homes in the winter and it didn't seem important at the time decide that they must have a pool during the following summer. Sometimes a pool can be added to the home they bought, but often that won't work because the contractors can't get large equipment into the backyard without destroying the neighbor's yard. So to get a pool, they have to sell and buy another home. Like condo regrets, these mistakes are great for Florida real estate agents but costly for Mr. and Mrs. Jones.

If you and your family never swim, and never want to

go in the water, well a decision is easy for you. If you are going to live in Florida twelve months out of the year, then a pool home will probably be the right choice. If you will be living near the beach and think that will be a great pool substitute, you may find overcrowding, lack of or expensive parking, excessive litter, rude sunbathers with music blaring and beach closings due to contaminated water from high bacteria counts from fecal matter, red tide and other reasons are a lot to put up with on an ongoing basis.

I can tell you this, any home I would buy in Florida for full-time living or even living six and six, would have a caged pool and in-ground spa combo. This doesn't have to be expensive because most people don't need a large pool, but the in-ground spa is a lot easier to get in and out of than a portable one. Like above ground pools, portable spas and hot tubs can be a turn off for many buyers after seeing the in-ground ones that have a waterfall that spills over into the pool providing a soothing sound. Many people use the hot tub more than the pool, especially in the winter months. Even if you don't use it very often, the atmosphere a caged pool and spa with a waterfall makes being in your backyard more pleasant. In normal market conditions, a caged pool home will sell faster and often for more money than the regular pool during the humid months.

Home Size Does Matter

What size home should you buy or build? That depends upon how much time you plan on spending there. If this will be your only home, it should be large enough to be comfortable year round. The following are some tips that may help you whether you will be living in Florida full time or living the life of a sixer.

Florida homes are often described as a 3/2/2. This means it has: 3 bedrooms/2 baths/2 car garage.

You may be spending a larger portion of your time outdoors while living in Florida. Grilling and dining outside daily is common in the less humid months. Homes with outdoor kitchen areas are becoming more common even in moderately priced properties. There is a trend toward more elaborate screened outdoor areas complete with everything you would normally find in a family, living or rec room. Many find they do not need as much inside living square footage as they had up north, especially if they are retiring. I've sold more properties for retired people in Florida that bought too big when they first arrived and wanted to downsize than the reverse. Many said it took too much time to clean, and they rarely used most of it.

The most desirable Florida homes have at least 3 bedrooms and two full baths. If there are just two in your family, this allows you to have a home office and a separate bedroom and bath set up to accommodate overnight guests. Many modern FL homes have a large master bedroom suite and two smaller bedrooms, which works fine for most people. In most areas of Florida, two bedroom homes are slow sellers, as are homes with 4 bedrooms or more.

A two car garage at a minimum is what most buyers desire because most Florida homes will not have a basement. Even if you only have one car, the other bay will come in handy for keeping bikes, lawn equipment and a place to cram your outdoor furniture when a hurricane is approaching.

Starting in the late eighties to early nineties, most new homes were built with cathedral ceilings and open floor plans. These homes can appear much larger than older homes with only flat 8' ceilings of the same size. A 1250 sq ft 3/2/1 built in the 1970s with flat eight foot ceilings and a long hall leading to three bedrooms may seem too small and cramped. A new home of that same size with cathedral ceilings and an open split floor plan will seem much larger and more livable. A split floor plan has a master bedroom suite (with its own bathroom and walk-in closet) on one side of the home with the other two bedrooms all the way over on the other side of a mostly open living, dining and kitchen area. Split floor plans are ideal for separating the kids, office or guests from your sleeping quarters.

A 1250 sq ft 3/2/2 split floor plan will probably be the minimum that is comfortable for full time living for two people. If you're on a tight budget, a newer home of this size with higher ceilings and open floor plan with screened lanai and pool can be very livable, and a good economical sixer home.

What size home will be right for you? Start by looking at smaller square footage new or almost new homes because they will have the best floor plans, and gradually work your way up in size. You will eventually find what size feels comfortable. Avoid letting an agent take you to the very largest home first because any home you look after that may feel too small, when it fact it may be the right size for you. Buying the costliest home you can afford may put more money in an agent's pocket, but you will probably be happier long term with a home that is the right size for you.

Vacant homes tend to look smaller than furnished homes of the same size. Vacant rooms look smaller than when they are furnished. That's why model homes are almost always furnished. Model homes decorated by a professional with expensive furnishings sell homes, but your home won't look like that unless you spend what the builder did.

Be aware that there is a whole industry of furniture manufacturers that make dining tables, sofas, etc. just a little smaller than normal size to "stage" brand new homes. Many builders put this furniture in their models to make them appear larger than they are. You may encounter model homes impeccably furnished throughout and the garage finished into a sales office. The sales office will have regular furniture where you will be encouraged to sit, but not inside the rest of the home because you may realize the furniture is smaller than normal.

Getting the best home for you at the best price

Get a list of the homes that match your criteria, like

3/2/2 pool homes under $xxx,xxx in the area you prefer. Look at as many homes as you can stand, all in one day. Start with the lowest price home first and work your way up in price. While going up in price, the homes should be newer, larger and nicer. Make notes like "way too small" while noting the square footage because this may help you avoid wasting time looking at similar small homes as you work your way up in price.

Go up in price until you find a home that will be ideal. Check the list to see if there are any homes of similar age, size and price on the list that you should look at. Resist looking at anything much larger or more expensive once you find a home that will work just fine. Continuing to look at ever more expensive homes increases the chances of indecision and can lead to buying a more costly home than you really need and regrets later.

Flood Zones

According to FEMA (The Federal Emergency Management Association) all homes are in a flood zone, because anywhere it can rain, it can flood. What matters most is if you are in a low, medium or high risk flood zone. If you are in a high risk zone and get a mortgage, you will be required by the lender to get flood insurance in addition to homeowners insurance. If you are paying cash, you can't be forced to buy flood insurance, but in a high risk zone in Florida, it would probably be foolish not to. If a home is damaged by flooding, regular homeowner insurance won't cover any of the damages.

Building codes in Florida have changed drastically in the last couple of decades in an attempt to minimize the damage done by tropical storm force winds and flooding. The new codes require builders to raise the base elevation of the floor of the home many feet above the surrounding ground in most areas. In the old days, a builder would just come out and pour a slab and start building.

In many areas, you'll see a newer home built right next to a much older home. Even though both homes may be ranches, you can see that the new home sits up much higher off the road than the older home. In fact, the older home's front door may seem to be almost the same level as the road, whereas the newer home's door is many feet higher. If you had a flash flood with a foot of water, you can see how the older home could be completely flooded, but the newer home would not be affected at all.

This is why an older Florida home may cost less to buy, but can cost a lot more to own because of the higher insurance premiums. When getting insurance in a higher risk flood zone, most times an insurance agent can't even give you a quote unless you can provide an elevation certificate that shows the home's base floor elevation. Some counties have the elevation of homes, especially newer ones, listed on their website from when the home was built because it was part of the required permitting process. The seller may already have one from when they bought or built the home. Have your realtor ask for it, as it could save you a little cash. You may have to pay surveyors to provide one if you can't get one any other way. The lower the elevation, the higher the risk and cost of insurance.

Get a homeowners insurance quote from an insurance agent before you sign an offer on a home. You don't want to be contracted to buy an older home to save money, only to find it will cost you $500 a month extra to just insure it. You would have been better off buying a newer, larger home with a lower insurance cost, because the total monthly cost would have been the same.

Market Price Warning

Florida's economy and real estate market is typical of high growth states and may be far different than what you are accustomed to. Sometimes it's isolated from, or more affected by, recessions felt by the rest of the US. The housing market is usually in some stage of a boom or bust cycle. As a realtor selling homes for over 12 years there, I have seen $99,900 homes that were worth $200,000 four years later. I have also seen brand new homes that were sold for $239,000, worth only $100,000 three years later.

If you buy in Florida when times are good, there is a good chance that you are buying near or at the top of the market. That's OK if you will be living there a long time, through many up and down markets. It's not good if you buy near the top of a good market and then have to sell near the bottom of a bad one.

In recessions, home prices usually just stall in the northern U.S. but they almost always will drop in Florida. Often the drop is fast and painful. You may find that the home you bought is worth $100,000 less than what you paid. This is a big hit if you paid cash but could be even worse if you took out a mortgage. What happens when you are absolutely miserable in Florida and want out, but you owe $200,000 on a house that's only worth $100,000? Do you sell and write a check at closing for $100,000 plus closing costs to get rid of it? Or do you continue to live in an area you hate for years, waiting for the value to go back up?

Do you rent it and become a landlord from a thousand miles away? What happens if the tenants stop paying, don't move, and trash your home while living there without paying? I have seen people cry when showing me what tenants did to their home when they decided to rent rather than sell in a down market. Or do you just move and stop paying the mortgage and get foreclosed on? The bank may get a judgment against you for the difference and chase you with it for years. I have seen all of this happen many times.

Those are all terrible options, of course. If you are young, you could have time to recover from financial setbacks. Later in life, coming back from such setbacks may not be possible. If you are buying a home for full-time Florida living, extra care should be taken when purchasing because you may be at higher risk of selling in a depressed market, and may have to sell that home in order to move on.

Become Immune to Price Drops

Sixers can be less concerned with where real estate is when they buy. Chances are they'll keep the place in Florida for years, through up and down cycles and be completely unaffected. If you do decide to sell, you'll more likely be able to choose the best time, because you won't be as motivated as a full timer who's had it with Florida.

If you want to be a full-time Florida resident and absolutely love it and will stay here long term, you will also be immune to yo-yo markets. If you have done your research, rented and tested living there, and loved it, then you may be immune to the market as well. You can buy a home in paradise regardless of market conditions and enjoy the Florida lifestyle. You can watch the economy soar and sink. It won't bother you at all, because you aren't selling. If you could live in Florida forever, but do decide to sell, you can pick the best time because you're in no particular hurry. You know that if now is not a good time, you can just wait a few years and it probably will be a great time to sell.

This immunity applies mainly to those with investment or retirement income, or in fields of employment that are unaffected by the economy, like health care positions seem to be. Florida's boom and bust economy is more of a risk to those that need to work to earn a living. Losing your job during a Florida bust can be devastating. During the great recession of 2008, Florida's unemployment rate soared far above the national average and at the same time home values plummeted by up to 60%.

I hope you've enjoyed reading this book and that it helps you make the best decision possible about Florida living.

Helpful Resources

Asset Protection

AssetProtectionBook.com- Best website pertaining to the subject, and you'll find their famous list of how the 50 states of the US rank. Definitely worth a look to compare the state you are now in to states you may be considering moving to.

The Asset Protection Book, the book written by the attorneys from the website mentioned above. Available from online booksellers like Amazon and through bookstores.

State of Florida Official Website

MyFlorida.com - This is the place to go to learn everything you could possibly need to know, like how to get a driver's license, where to get your car registration, and to check if your real estate agent is actually licensed and if she has any disciplinary actions doled out to her. If you decide to move to the sunshine state, this site will help you become a citizen in good standing because you will learn how soon after your arrival you have to register your cars, get a driver's license, etc.

Homes/Real Estate/Realtors

RonStack.com - My real estate broker/agent referral service website. Want to get the best possible home in Florida? Then only work with a great agent that cares more about you than their commission. Contact me through my website and my team will select a highly qualified agent to help you with your purchase anywhere in Florida. We can also put you in touch with the best agents to help you sell the home you're in now no matter where in the world you're located. This service is provided to you absolutely free, as we are compensated through long standing industry agreements.

An additional benefit of using this service is that you will be provided with my cell phone number for advice or help if you ever run into a problem during your move. Why risk using a bad agent when making one of the most important moves of your life when you can get help from my referral service for free?

Hurricanes

www.nhc.noaa.gov - The National Hurricane Center - The go-to site for information of all kinds on hurricanes from preparing a hurricane kit to live tracking and predicted paths and impacts of live hurricanes. This is the site that I checked on a regular basis when hurricanes were heading toward Florida because I could get updated information before it was available from news sources such as TV. This is where the TV meteorologist gets their information.

Research

Researching Specific Cities/Towns In Florida And Nationwide - A must-see free site provided by the U.S. Census Bureau. You can do some of your due diligence here before deciding to move to any particular city or town. Everything you could ever want to know about what kind of people live in an area including age groups, education levels, employment, etc. Florida specific data plus drop down menu to research any Florida county or town is here:

http://quickfacts.census.gov/qfd/states/12000 .html

Index

Alphabetical Index

Made in the USA
Monee, IL
05 April 2021

64840651R00095